ORBIS CONNOISSEUR'S LIBRARY

POTTERY

MALCOLM HASLAM

ORBIS PUBLISHING LONDON

Contents

Designed and produced by Harriet Bridgeman Limited

Printed in Italy by IGDA, Novara
SBN 0 85613 120 2

The evolution of a craft

Pottery is universal. The basic elements used in its manufacture – earth, water, fire – are available wherever man exists: they are as much the rudiments of human life as they are of pottery. The uses of pottery embrace a wide range of human activities, and in this respect, too, it may legitimately be identified with our existence.

But the creation of pottery is not only to be associated with the simple skills and basic needs of man. Refinements in the processes of manufacture and decoration have made it a sophisticated art-form. The potter's powers of artistic expression have often met the most searching demands of intellectual contemplation.

If pottery is an art, however, the artist-potter has to share the process of creation with forces which he must learn to control. The clay on the fast-spinning wheel finds its own shape through centrifugal force; the quality of the glaze, the shade and intensity of the colours used in decoration, is dependent on minute variations in the heat and atmosphere of the kiln. At different times in the history of pottery, the potter has either attempted to negate these factors by developing a technical expertise which eliminates the accidental, or he has tried to exploit the vagaries of the medium and, with just as sophisticated techniques, has allowed the wheel and the kiln to express themselves in his finished vessel. The balance between these two attitudes determines the style of the pottery and reflects not only the potter's temperament but also, very often, the nature of the society and the epoch to which he belongs.

A society also has more direct ways of imposing its features on the pottery it produces. Particular needs of people govern the forms their pottery takes and also, sometimes, its decoration. From the Japanese tea-ceremony of the Middle Ages to twentieth-century mass production, ritual or economy have affected the creations of the potter. The other crafts practised by a society also help to determine the nature of its pottery: the earliest Egyptian vessels are thought to have resulted from the accident of a clay-lined basket being burned and for some time the Egyptian potter followed the form of the basket and decorated his pots with incised patterns in imitation of its woven rushes. The interaction between pottery and metalwork has often been a factor in the evolution of their styles: from when metal was only used by the aristocratic classes, pottery shapes have emulated those of bronze and silver.

The earliest known ceramic industry dates from around 6500 BC. It was situated in west central and southern Anatolia, where it was carried on by cave-dwelling communities. Over the next five thousand years, the potters of the ancient Near East developed most of the rudimentary techniques of pottery, which have since been refined but hardly superseded. Many early Near Eastern ceramics show evidence of having been baked in a fire covered with earth or dung; this method took much longer than the open hearth, but the even heat resulted in a far higher proportion of pots being baked successfully.

The low firing temperature of early ceramics meant that the vessels often had a pitted surface and were more or less porous. To reduce this porosity, pots were smoothed while still wet so that imperfections were removed. Another method, in use before 5000 BC, was to paint the outside of the vessel with slip, a very highly refined clay; the slip surface was polished, or sometimes burnished, after firing. The pot was then more useful and its appearance was enhanced by the lustrous finish.

By about 4500 BC, the potters of northern Mesopotamia were producing a painted pottery of considerable merit. It has been called Samarra ware and was decorated with dark red or black paint on a matt cream slip. A similar tradition of decoration originated on the Persian plateau at about the same time. Before European influence was felt, painted decoration on Near Eastern pottery was mostly in geometrical patterns, sometimes relieved by stylised floral or animal forms.

Before 4000 BC, the vertical kiln was introduced in Mesopotamia and Persia, and it was being used in Egypt and Palestine by 3000 BC. The vertical kiln, in which the pottery is kept out of the fire itself, allows a greater and more even temperature and, by altering the draught, the potter has more control over the decoration of his products and can achieve a greater uniformity. Soon after 4000 BC, polychrome pottery was produced in northern Mesopotamia by applying different thicknesses of the same pigment to a vessel before firing.

The earliest pottery vessels were modelled by hand; probably the first turntables were of wood and have been

Above: Pottery storage-jar from Knossos, Crete, 1450–1400 BC (British Museum). Below: Pottery bowl; from Enkomi, Cyprus, Mycenaean, 1300–1200 BC (British Museum)

destroyed. A clay disc discovered at Ur dates from the period around 3000 BC, and stone wheels from the following millennium have been found in Palestine. A hand-turned wheel is shown in an Egyptian wall-painting of about 1900 BC.

The last of the fundamental techniques of pottery seems to have been developed soon after 2000 BC in Mesopotamia. A clay tablet has been discovered inscribed in Babylonian cuneiform with recipes for the production of copper-lead glazes and instructions for preparing the earthenware to take the glazes. Confirmation of the dating of these inscriptions was provided by the discovery in north Syria of earthenware vessels of the seventeenth to fourteenth centuries BC, covered with a spectacular blue-green glaze.

So, by the beginning of the first millennium BC, there were available to the potter the kiln and the wheel, and he had learnt to use slip, pigment and glaze. It had taken over half the known history of pottery to reach this stage. In the last three thousand years, using these basic discoveries, potters have reached heights of sophistication, both technical and intellectual; they have produced many varieties of ceramic art which fill the cases of our museums, and it is necessary to review the ceramic production of this later era in terms of a few salient points: summits of achievement surrounded by their foothills.

Greek pottery

Among the many contributions to the wealth of human experience made by the civilisation of classical Greece was its pottery. Around 1000 BC, a new level of technical excellence was achieved in the pottery created at Athens. The achievements of Mycenae and Crete during the second millennium BC were combined and developed in the new Attic pottery. The potting became more precise and the painted decoration more organized; motifs from marine and plant life were distributed in bands constructed with ruler and compass, supplemented by smaller bands of carefully drawn ornament. Before 750 BC, human figures, which had appeared only exceptionally on earlier Mycenaean vases reappeared and began to dominate the decoration.

Shortly after 700 BC, in Corinth, the black-figure technique was invented. The vessel of reddish clay was painted with figures and ornament in black slip. White and purple pigments were added to give a more lively effect and details such as limbs and clothing were incised in the black slip revealing lines of reddish clay. The technique was adopted by the Attic potters and a wide range of subjects was depicted: gods and goddesses, funerals, battles and games. The representation of more mundane activities, such as their equivalent of our dinner-parties, concerts and shopping expeditions, became increasingly popular.

The demands on the artist to show nuances of character and lifelike images had become too exacting by about the middle of the sixth century; the red-figure technique was developed in response. In this technique, the black slip was painted on all over the vessel up to the outline of the figures, which now appeared in the colour of the red clay. Instead of the artist having to incise details of the figures in the black slip silhouette, which necessarily restricted his fluency, he was able to use the black slip itself with which to brush in freely details of draperies, facial expressions and accessories. He was also able, by diluting the black slip with varnish, to modulate with shades of golden brown the contrast between black and red.

Pottery had become a painter's medium. As man became increasingly inquisitive about the nature of his universe, he learnt to render its appearance with ever greater verisimilitude on the walls of his buildings and on the surfaces of his utensils. Many subsequent cultures have found the pottery of the ancient Greeks so noble that they borrowed from it not only the concept of decorating their vessels with scenes from daily life, history or religion, but also its elegant forms – the amphora, the hydria and the krater.

The Orient

Further east, in China, sophisticated ceramics had already been produced for some time. By 1000 BC, Chinese potters were using glazes containing felspar, which is the flux used in the manufacture of porcelain. A fine, well vitrified stoneware, also with a felspathic content, was made during the Han dynasty (206 BC–AD 220). But it was during the T'ang period (AD 618–906) that the greatest advances were made in Chinese ceramics. The imperial capital at Ch'ang-an became the cultural centre of civilised Asia; commerce and conquest abroad made China receptive to foreign influences. In ceramic art the period is chiefly notable for the first porcelain manufacture, but in the field of pottery, too, considerable strides were taken. Among the most celebrated products of the T'ang potters was the three-coloured ware, a whitish earthenware decorated with green and amber-yellow lead glazes. At the same time, in south China, a grey-green glazed stoneware was made and decorated with moulded and finely incised ornament, most commonly of plants, birds and animals. This was the Yüeh celadon ware.

Below: Lion, Pottery figure with dappled green glaze. Chinese: T'ang dynasty (AD 618–906) (British Museum)

During the Sung period (AD 960–1279) further achievements were made in celadon ware, making it one of the most highly prized creations of Chinese ceramic art. In general, the ceramics of the Sung period were more varied and more stylish than those of the T'ang period. Artistic taste was considered at Court an enviable accomplishment, and potters thrived under discerning patronage. They became expert at controlling the atmosphere and temperature of the kiln. A wide range of colours was wrung from each glaze formula by means of varying the amount of oxygen in the kiln during firing, and the depth and viscosity of glazes were carefully calculated for aesthetic merit.

The shapes of T'ang pottery were refined during the Sung period and given great fluency of line; traces of their origin in the forms of metalwork disappeared. Sung shapes, which seem to belong to the world of flowers, have been imitated and emulated in both East and West ever since.

Korean and Japanese ceramics at this time were in general dependent on the current trends in China. Under the Koryo kings (918–1392), however, the Korean potters developed two types of national ware which bear comparison with contemporary Sung production. One is a grey-bodied ware covered in the 'kingfisher' glaze, the brilliance of which is more restrained than its Chinese counterpart. A second Korean ware of great technical distinction is a stoneware decorated with black and white slips inlaid under a celadon glaze.

The most notable ceramics produced in Japan in the period before the manufacture of porcelain became widespread were the vessels involved in the tea-ceremony. In accordance with the philosophy of this aesthetic ritual, the pottery was simply made, and its imperfections gained a perverse appreciation. There is a cultivated lack of sophistication about these wares which is characteristic of the Japanese mentality.

Oriental pottery was to have far less direct appeal to the European than Oriental porcelain. But the first attempts outside China to reproduce the whiteness and the glaze of Chinese porcelain are an important part of the history of pottery. They occurred in the Near East and bore fruit all over Europe.

Lustreware

In AD 750, the Persian Abbasids defeated the Umayyads after prolonged strife, during which the Chinese had taken the opportunity to undermine the authority of the Arab empire in its eastern provinces. The following year, the

Above: Illustration from 'Three Books of the Potters' Art' by Cipriano Piccolpasso, c.1556–9

Abbasids won victories over the Chinese and took twenty thousand prisoners. It is to this influx of Chinese ideas and skills that one may ascribe important developments in Mesopotamian pottery. A contributing factor was the prohibition under Islamic law of the use of vessels made of precious metals. Among other wares which emerged in Mesopotamia at this time was a lustre-painted pottery.

Tin-glazed pottery had been known in the ancient Near East; by the ninth century AD, it had been widely established. The fired earthenware is dipped into a suspension of lead glaze opacified by oxide of tin; the porous body absorbs the water and the glaze is left in an even deposit over the surface of the clay. On this white deposit the decoration is painted in metallic pigments which will stand the relatively high temperature required to fire and glaze:

Above: Dish from Deruta, early sixteenth century (Wallace Collection, London)

cobalt is used to give blue, manganese purple, copper green, antimony yellow and iron brick-red. The wares, carefully packed to protect them from smoke and fumes, are then fired in the kiln. The firing fuses the glaze and develops the colours of the painted design. Tin-glazed earthenware, made in emulation of the fine porcelains from China, accounts for by far the greatest part of luxury ceramics made in Europe until Böttger discovered the secret of porcelain at Meissen in the early eighteenth century.

Lustre decoration on tin-glazed earthenware is achieved by painting with silver or copper oxides over the tin glaze; the ware is then fired a third time. The technique probably originated in pre-Islamic Egypt, where lustre was painted on glass. From Iran the production of lustreware spread back to Egypt, where it blossomed during the Tulunid (868–905) and Fatimid (969–1171) dynasties. Grotesque birds, animals and human figures are the most popular motifs on Fatimid lustreware. The painting style is very refined and the lustre is a yellowish-greenish gold colour, darkening to a sombre yellow or brown at the end of the period. Sa'ad, whose name is signed on many vessels, was apparently the most famous artist working in this style.

During the eighth century, the Moors from North Africa colonized parts of the Iberian peninsular. In Spain the Muslim and Christian civilizations confronted each other and converged. Hispano-Moresque pottery, which dates from the twelfth century or earlier shows evidence of this convergence; the technique of producing this lustre-decorated tin-glazed ware presumably came from Fatimid Egypt as a result of trade. At first, the main centre of production in Spain was at Malaga.

One of the greatest achievements of the Andalusian potters was the large vases (about three and a half feet high), with handles shaped like wings, several of which have been found in the Alhambra Palace at Granada and have been subsequently named 'Alhambra' vases. To make pottery vases of such dimensions is a considerable technical feat; they were probably made, as comparable Chinese vases were, by joining together several cylindrical sections. Their narrow bases suggest that they are derived from Egyptian vases with pointed bases, which were stuck in the sand to make them stand upright.

Apart from many of its shapes and the technique of decorating it, Hispano-Moresque pottery betrays its Near Eastern origins in its decorative motifs and the inscriptions in Kufic script which many pieces bear. In the fourteenth century, potters from Andalusia migrated to the area of Valencia, which had been conquered from the Moors and restored to Christendom. Important factories were established at Manises and Teruel, and it is in the pottery produced at these places that romanesque and gothic stylistic elements appear. Wares are decorated with heraldic shields and with a wide range of birds and animals reminiscent of the art of northern Europe in their movement and vitality.

The simple Muslim shapes of the pottery produced at Malaga were, in the course of the fifteenth century, superseded at Valencia by more elaborate forms, sometimes produced on the wheel and sometimes from the mould. From Valencia the production of lustre pottery spread to Aragon and Catalonia.

But already Valencia and Manises wares were becoming known beyond the Iberian peninsular. From Manises, potters travelled to France where they worked at Avignon, Bourges and Poitiers. The kings of Aragon, Martin I and Alphonse V, sent examples of Manises ware to their dominions in Naples and Sicily.

Maiolica and faience

There had been Italian pottery with painting on a tin glaze since the eleventh century, and the Crusades had brought about a certain amount of Arab influence.

The decoration of these early Italian wares, of which production was widespread throughout Umbria, Latium, Tuscany, the Romagna and the Adriatic coast, was largely geometrical with figures treated with the stiffness and formality of Byzantine art. With the Florentine Renaissance in the first half of the fifteenth century, there emanated from Tuscany a style of decoration in which motifs from classical architecture were common.

The decisive development in Italian tin-glazed pottery was the arrival from Spain of the Hispano-Moresque ware of Valencia. Trade between the coastal cities of Italy, from Genoa in the north to Naples in the south, and the Mediterranean ports of Christian Spain had been growing steadily. The island of Majorca was a staging-post on this trade route and gave its name, 'maiolica', to the Italian version of Hispano-Moresque pottery. The latter was copied by manufacturers in Tuscany and the Romagna, who developed a great richness and variety of decoration in the 'gothic-floral' style.

The colours they used were clear and brilliant, and the subject-matter consisted of formalized foliage in elaborate patterns. Additional motifs were the Persian palmette and the 'peacock-feather eye'. The latter, one of the greatest *tours de force* in the whole history of painted decoration on pottery, was particularly prevalent on the ware produced

Centres of manufacture of tin-glazed earthenware

at Faenza in the last half of the fifteenth century, where the motifs had political significance. It was used by the potters as a mark of homage to Cassandra Pavoni (*'pavone'* being the Italian word for 'peacock'), the mistress of Caleotto Manfredo, the lord of Faenza.

The wide range of motifs and the richness of decorative effect achieved by the Faenza artists may perhaps be seen best in the tiles covering the whole floor of the chapel of S. Sebastian in the church of S. Petronio in Bologna, which were laid in 1487. These were from the workshop of Petrus Andrea, who is portrayed on one of them.

From a style of decoration which incorporated classical motifs, it was a natural development, following the course of Italian renaissance art, that pictorial representations of classical, mythological and religious scenes should become dominant. The illusionistic virtuosity of the renaissance fresco- and panel-painter was, in the first decades of the sixteenth century, applied to pottery. Artists from Faenza were the pioneers in this field. Their painterly treatment is known as the '*istoriato*' style and came to include imitations of the grotesque motifs which were used in the decoration of the Vatican apartments by Raphael, who was inspired in his turn by the fresco decorations found in the ruins of classical buildings.

At Deruta, near Perugia, maiolica was decorated with lustre-painted ornament. The richest lustreware, however, was made at nearby Gubbio, where the characteristic colours were gold, ruby-red and silver.

A later style of maiolica which also appeared first (*c.*1540) at Faenza is called '*compendiario*'. Most of the piece is left unpainted, the tin glaze becoming thicker and of an intense whiteness. Designs were more sketchy and carried out in a limited range of colours – cobalt-blue, yellow and orange. The enormous amount of this ware which was produced and exported gave the name of the town to tin-glazed pottery in France and England (faience), and Germany (fayence).

The faience industry in France originated in the work done on the decoration of the Duc de Berry's *châteaux* at Bourges and Poitiers between 1332 and 1338 by a certain

Jehan of Valencia. At about the same time, Muslim potters expelled from Catholic Spain settled in the Narbonne region of southern France. In the sixteenth century, Italian maiolica potters arrived in France and soon taught their art to local craftsmen. Masséot Abaquesne, the first great master of French faience, probably worked in Italy before setting up his workshops in Rouen in 1526. Rouen wares were to be celebrated over the next two centuries. An important centre of production was also established at Nimes by the Huguenot potter Antoine Sigalon.

In Germany, the manufacture of tin-glazed tiles for stoves flourished in Nuremberg and the south Tyrol from the beginning of the sixteenth century, although the technique was not new. The decorative motifs employed are sometimes reminiscent of Venetian maiolica decorations.

Other centres of faience production in Germany, at Frankfurt and Hanau as well as potteries at Norwich and Lambeth in England and several centres in Spain, owe their establishment to the enterprise of faience manufacturers from Antwerp, the busiest commercial city in Europe during the sixteenth century. In 1512 Guido Andriesz, a potter from Casteldurante in Italy, set up a pottery in Antwerp. The Andriesz family and the family of Floris were responsible for the dissemination of maiolica manufacture across northern Europe and in Spain.

Delftware

By the end of the sixteenth century the production of maiolica at Haarlem had been established. This factory was also founded by an Antwerp potter. When, at the beginning of the seventeenth century, two shiploads of Ming blue-and-white porcelain arrived at Amsterdam, the Chinese ware immediately provoked attempts at imitation. Only a few pieces of Ming blue-and-white had reached Europe overland during the sixteenth century. Very quickly polychrome decoration at the Haarlem factory gave way to the blue alone. The potting became finer in emulation of porcelain; the drawing became more delicate; and Chinese shapes superseded the metalwork or Muslim shapes of Italian maiolica.

Below: Posset-pot, Lambeth. (Ashmolean Museum, Oxford; Warren Collection)

The production of blue-and-white tin-glazed pottery quickly became a national industry of the Netherlands, centred on Delft. At the Delft potteries two further technical innovations were made. Outlines were drawn in manganese purple on to the unglazed clay; as a result the drawing of the designs became livelier and stronger. Second, outside surfaces were finished with a lead glaze to give the ware the glossy appearance of Chinese porcelain.

Early Delftware was a close imitation of Chinese porcelain but, by the 1690s, baroque forms began to appear. Large vases and cisterns, some over three feet high, following European shapes were made for William and Mary's Hampton Court Palace. Their designs were based on those by Daniel Marot, the architect to the Dutch Court. Landscapes and designs after etchings were other decorative subjects which deviated from the style of the Chinese originals. But imitation continued and some Delftware was decorated in polychrome after the Chinese porcelain of the Transitional Period (*c.*1640) between Ming and Ch'ing.

Delftware influenced a greater part of the painted tin-glazed pottery produced in northern Europe throughout the late seventeenth and the early eighteenth centuries. In England it was imitated at three main centres – London, Bristol and Liverpool. In 1661, Dutch religious refugees established a pottery at Hanau, and soon German faience production was dominated by the Chinese-Delft influence; Frankfurt, Berlin and Potsdam were the main centres.

Under Louis XIV, France was engaged in a succession of costly wars, and edicts were promulgated in 1689 and 1709 ordering the melting down of all gold and silver vessels. This strongly promoted the faience industry: old factories flourished and new ones were opened. Most decoration was in blue or in the *famille verte* and *famille rose* colours of Chinese porcelain. Designs were for the most part of Chinese inspiration, but the rococo style of paintings by Watteau and Boucher influenced decoration in the second half of the eighteenth century. Rouen, Moustiers, Strasbourg, Marseilles and Lorraine were all centres of production.

By 1750 there had been for nearly a thousand years a tradition of tin-glazed earthenware decorated with high-temperature colours. Starting in the Near East as a result of contact with Chinese culture, it accounted for the greater part of the luxury pottery produced in Europe from the middle of the fifteenth century to the middle of the eighteenth. From about 1600, a fresh look at Chinese porcelain brought about another great flowering of the tradition at Delft and elsewhere. Only with the beginning of the manufacture of porcelain in Europe itself was the tin-glaze tradition threatened. That, and the increasing cost of mining tin as the mines became deeper, together with improvement in the quality of lead-glazed wares, changed the course of pottery's development.

Lead-glazed pottery

Even during the period of tin-glazed pottery's greatest success, a high level of technical quality and decorative effect had been achieved with lead-glazed ware. In Italy

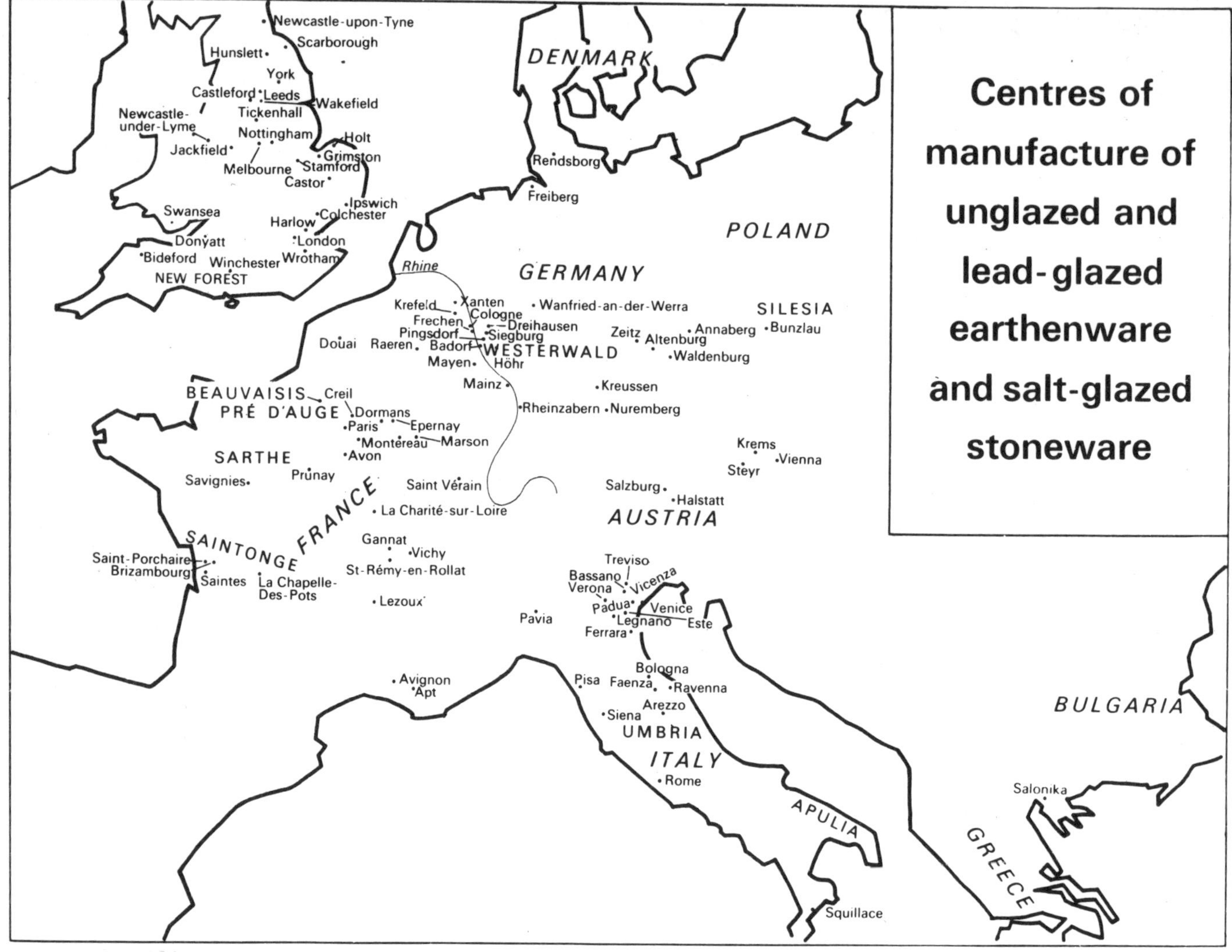

Centres of manufacture of unglazed and lead-glazed earthenware and salt-glazed stoneware

slip-decorated pottery was produced, known as '*mezza-maiolica*'. It is characterized by its contrast of red and white produced by incised decoration through white slip to the red clay beneath. Coloured glazes were also used, giving a polychrome effect.

In France, despite the popularity of faience, pottery decorated with coloured slip which was the traditional product of the French potters continued to be widely used, even as princely gifts. The pottery was often impressed with low-relief decoration in the form of masks, coats of arms, foliage, figures, motifs from gothic architecture, and inscriptions in gothic lettering; such pieces were often green-glazed.

Fine examples were produced at Beauvais, where also statues of horsemen and musicians were manufactured; they were used to cap the finials on roofs.

Particularly accomplished were the potters from the area of Poitou who made the *Henri Deux* (Henry II) ware, probably at Saint-Porchaire; this was a great feat of technical virtuosity in the field of slip-decorated pottery. The manufacture of this ware was limited to the years between *c.*1530 and *c.*1570, but in that short period from heavy shapes decorated with horizontal bands of repeating ornaments there developed more elaborate pieces, often of an architectonic character, decorated with intricate renaissance patterns similar to those found on contemporary buildings. Saint-Porchaire earthenware was made from a fine-grained clay with a high silica content which stayed white on firing and was covered with a transparent glaze. The ornament is precisely painted in black and different tones of brown slip. Sometimes a few touches of other colours were added.

Another French achievement of the sixteenth century, also in slipware, was the 'rustic' pottery of Bernard Palissy. He decorated his pottery with polychrome glazes, his handling of which was remarkably refined, and to it he applied snakes, lizards, frogs, fishes, shells and foliage, which were cast in slip from the life and naturally reproduced. His style relates closely to the mannerist sculpture of the Fontainebleau School. The production of the Palissy workshops was considerably augmented by many imitators, but the lively figures made at Avon, near Fontainebleau, and the elaborate roof-finials from Le Pré d'Auge in Normandy, although technically and stylistically related, stand on their own merits.

Sixteenth- and seventeenth-century lead-glazed pottery production in Germany was largely conditioned by the manufacture of tiled stoves. From the sixteenth century, stove-tiles were modelled in relief with figures in niches or subjects such as myths and allegories. Particularly successful were the tile decorations modelled in the workshops of the Leupold family at Nuremberg. Their tiles were glazed black and the modelling was effectively heightened by a restrained use of gold. The jugs created by the Preuning family, decorated with contemporary religious and political celebrities, were also made at Nuremberg. They were coloured with green, brown, manganese-purple, yellow and white glazes which were prevented from running together by an ornamental pattern of raised lines. The figures were modelled in relief.

Stoneware in Europe

The more significant contribution to the development of pottery made by Germany at this time was the production of a fine salt-glazed stoneware. This stoneware was produced from a clay which has a high silicic acid content which, when fired at a high temperature, vitrifies. Lead glazes cannot withstand the required heat so the ware is salt glazed; the salt is thrown into the kiln and the soda combines with the silica and alumina in the clay, producing a thin glassy film over the surface of the vessel. The glaze could be given colour by means of a wash of vitrifiable brown clay.

Stoneware production was centred on the Rhineland with its rich deposits of clay on the slopes of the Westerwald, at Siegburg, Frechen, Raeren and to the south of Aachen. Cologne functioned as an *entrepôt* for the industry and the river facilitated export to the Netherlands, England, Scandinavia and France.

Rhenish stoneware was brought to its technical and artistic peak during the sixteenth century, after the gothic had been largely superseded by the renaissance style in the region of Cologne. Its characteristic forms were bellied jugs, beakers with flared mouths, the *Schnelle* (a tall, tapering tankard), the Bellarmine (a jug decorated with a bearded mask below the spout) and the *Schnabelkanne* (a richly decorated, spouted jug with cylindrical neck and body sections). Relief decoration was of considerable artistic merit and probably owed much of its inspiration to the graphic artists of Nuremberg, such as Peter Flötner and Hans Sebald Beham, whose work was widely circulated and readily available to the potters.

In the 1630s, the Thirty Years' War destroyed or brought to a standstill many of the potteries at Siegburg and Raeren and new workshops were established on the Westerwald at Höhr and Grenzhausen. The typical Westerwald jug has an ovoid body rising directly from the foot-ring and a narrow cylindrical neck. They were decorated with a regular diaper of stamped floral and leaf motifs. Cobalt-blue and manganese-purple glazes give them colour, incised lines preventing the glazes from running together. This decorative technique is known as *'Blauwerk'* and is still practised today.

Stoneware was made at many other centres all over Germany, and also at Beauvais in France. In England there were spasmodic attempts from the second half of the sixteenth century to produce a stoneware to compete with imports from Germany, but not until the 1670s did John Dwight's Fulham Pottery begin production. It may well have been in an attempt to make porcelain that Dwight, previously an ecclesiastical lawyer, produced fine, almost white stoneware, which was sometimes partially translucent. His bottles, on which black and white clays were sometimes mingled to give a marbled effect over the brown salt-glazed stoneware, were decorated with applied moulded reliefs. In light grey stoneware, Dwight made small, finely potted mugs and figures; being salt glazed, the details of the modelling were not lost under a thick lead glaze.

Dwight had taken out patents for his processes of manufacture in 1671 and 1686, and in 1693 he took legal action against potters who, he claimed, were infringing them. Among those indicted were members of the Wedgwood family from Burslem in Staffordshire, John Morley from Nottingham, who made a fine brown stoneware often embellished with pierced ornaments, and the brothers John and David Elers, who were silversmiths from Germany.

The Elers brothers had worked under John Dwight and subsequently settled at Bradwell Wood in Staffordshire, where they made, as Dwight did also, unglazed red stoneware in imitation of Yi-hsing redware which was commonly imported from China at the time. Red stoneware was also produced in England between 1740 and 1780.

Eighteenth-century Staffordshire

The establishment of potteries in Staffordshire was due to the particularly favourable conditions there. A variety of different clays were available and coal was plentiful in the region. Important pottery was produced at other centres, including York, where Francis Place produced stoneware mugs of great refinement, setting standards of technical excellence the Staffordshire potters were soon rivalling.

The eighteenth century also saw the production in Staffordshire of sophisticated slipware. Pottery decorated with trailed and spotted white slip had been produced during the early seventeenth century at Wrotham, Kent, but more significant slipware dishes were made in North Staffordshire from the time of the Restoration (1660). The slip painting there, particularly the work of Charles Toft, was elaborate and accomplished. In about 1710, Staffordshire slipware was made in moulds into which the main lines of the design were incised; these lines appeared as ridges on the pottery which formed compartments for variously coloured slips.

Another method of decoration developed in Staffordshire was to comb different coloured slips while they were still liquid into 'feather' or 'arcade' patterns. Marbling effects were produced by pressing together differently coloured clays.

A determining factor in the evolution of creamware was the manufacture of white salt-glazed stoneware, which was originally produced at the very end of the seventeenth century. By the 1720s, in order to achieve greater whiteness, the grey stoneware was given a surface wash of white Devonshire clay. The next step was to introduce ground flint as well as the Devonshire clay into the body of the ware; it then had greater whiteness and less weight.

This ware was produced in great quantities around the middle of the eighteenth century. Much of it was given a coating of lead glaze, which was probably introduced in an attempt to rival the new creamware.

White salt-glazed stoneware was usually decorated with moulded reliefs. Incised decoration was also used, the lines of the design often being filled with cobalt-blue, a colour which was also often used to accentuate the moulded reliefs. From about 1745, the ware was made, often in elaborate and quaint shapes, from plaster-of-Paris moulds by means of the technique known as 'slip-casting'. The plaster-of-Paris mould, which was shaped from a stoneware die, was filled with slip. The water was absorbed into the mould and a thin layer of clay left. This was repeated until the thickness of the walls gave the vessel its required strength. The process allowed a great number of the same shape of vessel to be produced, and also ensured a remarkable thinness.

The development of creamware was the result of a convergence in the first half of the eighteenth century of the techniques involved in the manufacture of, on the one side, lead-glazed slip-decorated earthenware and, on the other, salt-glazed stoneware. Creamware was the culmination of the European potters' persistent endeavours to produce an alternative to porcelain, the production of which was costly and often subsidized. That the new body was achieved in England was due in part to colonial trade, by means of which tea-drinking had become by the end of the seventeenth century a widespread habit. The Staffordshire potters had responded to the greatly increased demand for an inexpensive china of drawing-room quality.

Creamware was the natural development from these established Staffordshire wares. At first it was made from the same ingredients and by practically the same process as the stoneware, except that it was fired at a low temperature and given only a lead glaze. In its more developed form, the ware was fired to a biscuit and then covered with a glaze containing ground flints and lead ore in powder form (*galena*). After refiring, the ware had a brilliant, cream-coloured appearance.

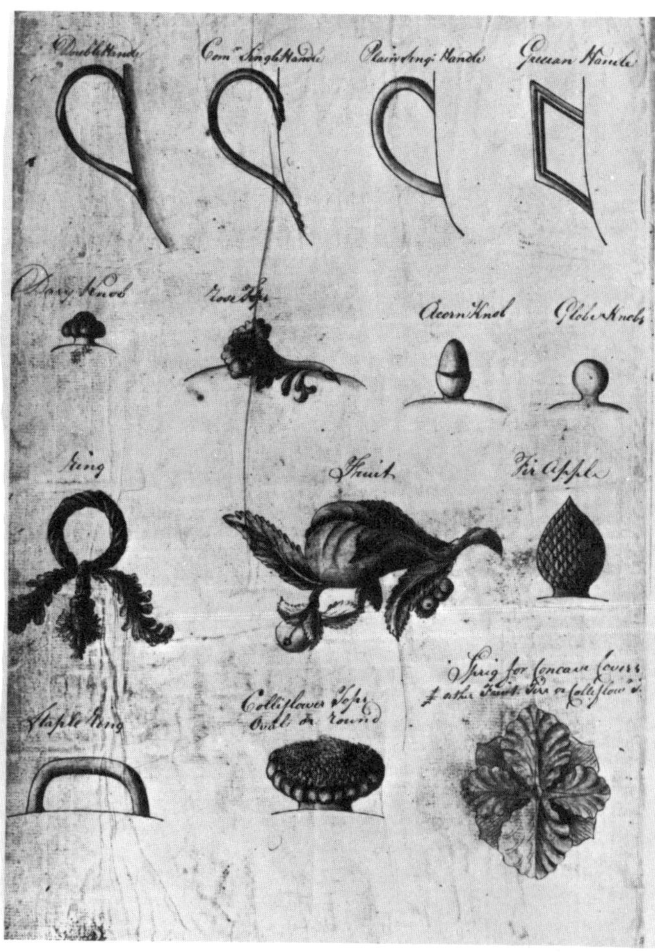

Technical proficiency in the manufacture of this ware was quickly acquired by several Staffordshire potters in the 1740s. Pieces were decorated with coloured glazes which were sometimes spattered and sometimes allowed to mingle ('tortoiseshell' ware). Under-glaze painting was also used to decorate creamware. Until 1760, its manufacture was carried on alongside that of salt-glazed stoneware, but after that date production of the latter declined.

Creamware was the ceramic material which was most ideally suited to meet the demand for refined tableware made by the new middle classes. Porcelain was too expensive and did not lend itself to the methods of series-production, the only means by which the required output could be reached. The potter to whose ceramic skills and entrepreneurial abilities the development of these methods must be ascribed was Josiah Wedgwood.

From 1754 to 1759 Wedgwood was a partner with Thomas Whieldon, at whose Fenton Hall pottery most forms of Staffordshire pottery were produced. Contemporaries regarded Whieldon as the genius of pottery, although it is not known for how many technical innovations he was himself responsible. Among those who worked with him in order to gain technical knowledge were Daniel

Top left: Fair Hebe Jug by J. Voyez, probably Ralph Wood's factory, 1788 (Victoria and Albert Museum, London). Bottom left: Page from Drawing Book No. 4 (Leeds City Art Gallery). Above: The Modelling Room at Etruria, as it appeared in the early 1790s

and William Greatbatch, Aaron Wood and Josiah Spode, as well as Wedgwood.

At Fenton Hall, Wedgwood took the opportunity to familiarize himself with the many different processes carried out there, and to investigate particularly coloured glazes. Early wares produced at Ivy House, where Wedgwood established his independent pottery, were mainly green-glazed teapots and other vessels in the form of various vegetables and fruits. These were made in lead-glazed earthenware, the pieces being supplied to Wedgwood in biscuit by William Greatbatch, an accomplished modeller.

From 1760 Wedgwood embarked on the manufacture of creamware and by 1765 had developed a new body, lighter in colour and weight than previous creamwares. He achieved this by constant research and experimentation, having different clays sent to him from remote places in Britain and abroad in order to assess their properties. Such investigations required accurate measuring devices and these Wedgwood's ingenuity provided. From 1764 to 1772, his pottery was at Burslem and the greatest part of the creamware he produced was sent for decoration to the transfer-printing works of Sadler and Green in Liverpool. The engravings, carefully selected by Wedgwood, were printed at first in black and then in black and red, purple being used for some landscapes.

At least from 1763, if not before, some of Wedgwood's creamware was decorated with enamelling by David Rhodes of Leeds, who subsequently took charge of Wedgwood's enamelling workshop in Little Cheyne Row, London. Rhodes' decoration was at first freely painted figures, landscapes and flowers; by 1770 his designs included neat, restrained border patterns.

Wedgwood's adoption of the neoclassical taste made fashionable by Robert Adam dates from the beginning of his association with Thomas Bentley, a Liverpool merchant of considerable taste and learning, who became his partner in 1769. Bentley supervized the London showroom for ornamental wares; he died in 1780.

In 1774 Empress Catherine of Russia commissioned Wedgwood to make a very large service in creamware. Each piece was enamelled in sepia with a specially painted landscape.

Other wares made by Wedgwood at his Etruria factory, which was opened in 1769, were basaltes (a black stoneware), red stoneware and jasper ware. The last was a finely potted stoneware originally made from clay coloured pale blue, dark blue, sage green, lilac, yellow or black by means of metallic oxides. After a few years the colour was applied in washes of slip. Classical subjects and ornamental motifs moulded in white clay were applied to the ware. Wedgwood's jasper ware was the sophisticated descendant of John Dwight's marble-glazed stoneware bottles, decorated with applied white reliefs. But the two wares represent totally different aesthetic and manufacturing backgrounds.

Wedgwood's achievement was to establish principles for the commercial production of pottery in an industrial age. A man of his day, he used advanced scientific aids for research into the most satisfactory clay bodies and glazes; he organized production according to the ideas of Adam Smith, whose *Wealth of Nations* (1776) argued the efficiency of the division of labour; he had his wares modelled and decorated in the style currently popular, not making any attempt to create a style of his own but at the same time never allowing his products to appear *démodé*; and finally, by assiduously pursuing the patronage of influential personalities and running a well-sited London showroom, he ensured the prestige of his products and their popularity.

Wedgwood's creamware was imitated in Britain and abroad. In Staffordshire, Turner, Neal and Wilson were potters who were soon producing a creamware of a quality comparable to Wedgwood's. The creamware made at the Leeds Pottery is pleasant in appearance and often original in shape. Staffordshire potters established creamware factories in France; there and elsewhere in Europe creamware was manufactured to compete with wares imported from England, which were much cheaper than locally produced porcelain and tin-glazed earthenware. Similarly, all over Europe and America transfer-printing became the commonest form of decoration on pottery, and it has remained so ever since.

Pottery as an industry

The industry which Josiah Wedgwood created in the last quarter of the eighteenth century has been sustained ever since by the steadily increasing number of people who find good-quality china appropriate to their social station. Methods of production and merchandizing have been improved but the same principles have persisted. Moreover, the production of the industry world wide has been dominated by very much the same wares. A lead-glazed white earthenware, moulded into shapes more or less derived from eighteenth-century porcelain or silver and decorated with transfer-printed designs in monochrome – such china is sold today by all good stockists. Among the particularly noted wares in this group were Josiah Spode's Stone China and Mason's Patent Ironstone. They were fired at higher temperatures than creamware and were almost porcellaneous. Many of the services produced by these firms were decorated by hand in enamel colours. F. R. Pratt, of Fenton, Staffordshire, refined the techniques of transfer-printing and from the 1840s produced china decorated with polychrome prints.

With the absorption of the country potter into the urban labour force, the demand arose for mass-produced, cheap wares. These were often gaily decorated so that their poor quality would not be so obvious, and much lustreware was made at most of the English pottery-producing centres, especially Sunderland. The tradition of figure-modelling which had flourished in the mid-eighteenth century with the work of Astbury and Whieldon, and which had reached its zenith in the work of the Wood family, was debased in the last two-thirds of the nineteenth century by the mass production of coarsely moulded and crudely coloured figures which, however, have some interest in their historical, ecclesiastical, literary, theatrical, criminal and sporting allusions. The whole range of cheap ornamental wares, produced in Europe and America during the nineteenth century and since, is very wide.

An increasing number of critics over the last one hundred and fifty years have demanded an original style of pottery. When the early Victorian neo-rococo style was seen, at the Great Exhibition of 1851, to have developed into a riot of flower, fruit, vegetable and animal forms treated with uncompromising naturalism, voices in Europe and America were raised in protest. The plea was made for greater discipline of design and a return to acknowledged masters of the past. This historicism was accompanied by a technical virtuosity which was admired by a society believing in its scientific and technological progress. A number of manufacturers produced a series of styles inspired by the past which in their brilliant emulation outdid the original in sophistication. Minton's of Stoke manufactured imitations of Palissy, *Henri Deux* ware (Saint-Porchaire) and Italian maiolica, called 'majolica' and decorated with coloured lead-glazes instead of being painted with pigment on tin-glaze, as was the original. Wedgwood, and lesser firms, followed Minton's lead. The achievement of reproducing industrially what was originally produced in studio conditions, of providing in sufficient quantity at a low enough price replicas of wares which had previously been available only to a Court, has sometimes been ignored.

Of the many historical and exotic styles which influenced the forms and decoration of nineteenth-century pottery, the most important was undoubtedly the Japanese. In many cases the assimilation of Japanese design went only so far as the imitation or the adoption of the well-known decorative motifs, such as storks and prunus blossom. But throughout Europe and America there were designers in the decorative arts who grasped the principles of Japanese design. The emphasis on purity of form and colour and on economy of decoration in the interests of aesthetic contemplation struck a chord in the sensibilities of many European and American designers of the later part of the nineteenth century who were dissatisfied with the art-historical didacticism and 'suggestive' ornament of contemporary ceramics. The 'art-pottery', as it was termed, which was produced in the spirit of Japanese art, was widely popular for a time and in turn provoked a response in the manufacture of useful wares.

One form the response took was the employment by the potters of recognized designers in other fields. In the last one hundred years, architects and industrial designers such as Christopher Dresser, Henry van der Velde, Peter Behrens and Keith Murray have all designed original ceramics. But it has been the opinion of many that originality and purity of form have been gained at the expense of a feeling for the material and for the creative process of pottery.

In the twentieth century, the artist-potter has denied most of the fundamental principles of the modern pottery industry. Rather than have a division of labour between designer, thrower and decorator, however accomplished they are in their respective roles, the artist-potter performs every part himself; this may be seen as one aspect of the expressionism which has been a major theme in the arts of the twentieth century. Related to this expressionism, is the artist-potters' desire not to go much beyond the simple techniques of the primitive potter, in whose work they claim to see an innocence and purity of soul; but to many the resulting crudity of their production seems affected.

Perhaps the greatest importance of the artist-potter to the future is his insistence on pottery as pottery. Throughout the history of this art-form the desire to emulate porcelain has not always been to the advantage of the potter's creation, even if it has produced masterpieces of technique and decoration. The tin-glazed tradition originated from admiration of Sung porcelain, and the endeavours of the eighteenth-century Staffordshire potters were to produce from their salt-glazed stoneware and lead-glazed earthenware a body to equal in hardness, whiteness and depth of glaze, the porcelain being produced by that time in Europe as well as the East.

Freed from this aspiration, pottery of the future will be able to exist as itself, in all its simple beauty.

MARKS ON POTTERY

ENGLAND

BRISTOL (Gloucester)
The Bristol Pottery,
1652-Pountney & Co.Ltd.,1849
earthenware

Bristol
Est.1652.
Pountney & Co Ld
England

mark of John Bowen,
delft-painter

Yf 1st Sept.
1761
Bowen - fecit.
in blue

about 1825

printed in blue

CASTLEFORD (Yorkshire)
c.1790-1820
Dunderdale, David
cream-coloured earthenware
and stoneware

DD&Co
CASTLEFORD
impressed

FULHAM (Middlesex)
1671-
salt-glazed stoneware
Dwight, John
probably 'Warland Dwight',
c.1740

WD
in blue

LIVERPOOL (Lancashire)
John Sadler & Guy Green,
printers 1756-1799

J. Sadler, Liverpl
Green, Liverpl

HERCULANEUM POTTERY,
c.1794-1841
bone-porcelain and
cream-coloured
earthenware

STAFFORDSHIRE

BRADWELL WOOD (Staffs)
Elers, John Philip and David,
late 17th and early 18th
century red stoneware

impressed

WOOD, AARON
(b.1717, d.1785)

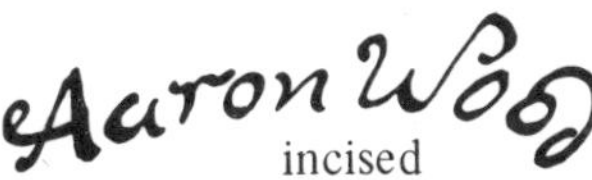

incised

WOOD, ENOCH (son,
b.1759, d.1840)
1784-

ENOCH WOOD
SCULPIST
E WOOD

WOOD, RALPH (brother of
Aaron Wood, b.1715, d.1772)
c.1770

R. WOOD

WOOD, RALPH (son,
b.1748, d.1795)
1772-c.1795

Ra. Wood
Burslem
all impressed

ETRURIA & BURSLEM
Wedgwood, Josiah,
b.1730, d.1795
1759-present
general pottery

WEDGWOOD
& BENTLEY

G 2430
W 2429
E 2431
H White

Wedgwood &
Bentley (1769-1780)

WEDGWOOD
& BENTLEY
W & B

TURNER, JOHN(d.1786)
general pottery
1784-
(potter to Prince of Wales)

TURNER
TURNER & CO

JOHNSON BROTHERS, Ltd.,
Hanley Pottery, 1883-
c.1913
1793-

Johnson Bros
England

MINTON'S Ltd.,
Thomas Minton and Herbert
Minton (son)
general pottery
1822-1836

780
in blue enamel

SPODE, JOSIAH,
b.1733, d.1797,
and family
c.1770

SPODE
impressed

Spode
impressed

FRANCE

ROUEN (Seine-Inferieure)
16th century
maiolica
'M A B' mark of Masseot
Abaquesne
faience, 1644-19th century

in blue

GERMANY

COLOGNE (Rhineland)
faience and porcelain
c.1770-early 19th century

in black
NF
in purple
KÖLN
impressed

KREUSSEN (nr Bayreuth)
stoneware
16th century

faience
early 17th century

Lorenz Speckner, dated 1618

·L·S·
L S

MEISSEN (nr. Dresden, Saxony)
marks found on Bottger's red
stoneware, c.1710-1720
or later

incised

RAEREN (nr. Aix-la-Chapelle, Rhineland)
c.1565-1600
stoneware
mark of Jan
Emens, c.1566-1594

HOLLAND

DELFT
(nr.Rotterdam)
red stoneware
c.1675-
18th century
Arij de Milde, 1680-1708

ITALY

CAFFAGGIOLO (nr. Florence)
early 16th century-
maiolica
' Jacopo ', artist

CASTEL DURANTE (renamed Urbania in
1635)
16th century-
maiolica
Nicola Pellipario, painter, dated 1521

DERUTA or DIRUTA
(Umbria)
c.1490-
maiolica

FAENZA (Emilia)
14th century-
maiolica
1480-1490
(This mark is now attributed to
Florence as an ownership mark)

GUBBIO (Duchy of Urbino)
c.1495
maiolica
various forms of Maestro
Giorgio's factory mark,
1519-1541

URBINO
c.1520-18th
century
maiolica

SPAIN

ALCORA (Valencia)
c.1726-
faience, c.1727-c.1785

A
in brown or black

Glossary of terms

Agate. A ware made in imitation of variegated natural stones such as agate by the use of different coloured clays.
Albarello. A cylindrical jar made to contain ointments and dry medicaments.
Amphora. A Greek jar with ovoid body and two handles intended primarily for storage.
Art-Pottery. Also called studio-pottery; decorative wares made by artist-potters at the end of the nineteenth century.
Basaltes. The name given by Josiah Wedgwood to his fine-quality black stoneware introduced in 1766.
Bianco-sopra-bianco. Decoration in white glaze-mixture.
Biscuit. Unglazed porcelain or, more rarely, pottery.
Cream-coloured earthenware. Also called creamware, a light-bodied earthenware with transparent (mainly lead-based) glaze: perfected in Staffordshire in about 1740–50, it began to supersede other tablewares in about 1760.
Cuerda seca. A method of separating glazes by outlines drawn in manganese and grease.
Delftware. Dutch tin-glazed earthenware named after the town of Delft: 'delftware' is thc English derivative.
Faience. Also called *fayence*, the term derives from the town of Faenza in Italy and describes tin-glazed earthenware; it has since been loosely applied to all types of white pottery.
Glaze. A shiny coating rendering pottery and porcelain impervious to liquids while lending brilliance to their surface; lead and salt glazes are applied to pottery.
Glost kiln. A kiln used for firing the glaze on a ware.
Granite ware. A creamware with a minutely speckled glaze resembling granite.
Jackfield ware. A black-glazed earthenware made in Shropshire *c.* 1750–75.
Jasper ware. A fine-grained unglazed stoneware perfected by Wedgwood in 1775; normally white, it could be stained with different metallic colours.
Krater. A deep Greek vessel for mixing wine or water, with two handles of varying shapes.
'Lambeth'. Often used to denote the London delftware potteries.
Maiolica. Tin-glazed earthenware.
Majolica. Misuse of the word 'maiolica' to describe colour-glazed wares of the mid-nineteenth century.
Pearl ware. A white variety, with a pearl-coloured glaze, of the cream coloured pottery ('Queen's Ware') introduced by Josiah Wedgwood in about 1779.
Queen's Ware. Cream coloured earthenware named in honour of Queen Charlotte, improved and marketed by Josiah Wedgwood.
Salt-glazed stoneware. A ware for which the glaze is formed by throwing common salt into the kiln when it reaches its highest temperature.
Sgraffiato. Decoration incised with a point, usually through a layer of slip.
Slipware. Pottery (normally lead-glazed) decorated with white or coloured slip.
Stoneware. A family of hard, high-fired wares, mostly salt glazed although some are left unglazed.
Tin glaze. Lead glaze made opaque by the addition of tin ashes.
Wasters. Pots, or fragments of pots, which have been spoiled and discarded.
Whieldon ware. Made in cream-coloured earthenware under a glaze splashed with metallic oxides to give mottled effects: made by Thomas Whieldon and others.

Bibliography

Charleston, R. J. (ed), *World Ceramics*, Paul Hamlyn, Feltham 1968

Cushion, J. P., and Honey, W. B., *Handbook of Pottery and Porcelain Marks*, Faber and Faber, London, third revised edition 1965

Honey, W. B., *European Ceramic Art from the End of the Middle Ages to about 1815* (2 vols), Faber and Faber, London 1959

Lane, A., *Style in Pottery*, OUP, London 1948

Savage, G., *Pottery Through the Ages*, Harmondsworth, London 1959

Wakefield, H., *Victorian Pottery*, Barrie and Jenkins, London 1962

Acknowledgements are due to the following for photographs used in this volume:

Art-Wood Photography, London: 20. BPC Publishing Ltd., London: 1, 4, 5, 10, 11, 17, 18, 19, 21, 22, 23, 24, 25, 26, 27, 28, 29, 30, 32, 33, 35, 36, 37, 40, 46, 47, 48, 59, 60, 61, 62, 63, 84, 85, 86, 87, 88, 92, 94, 95, 96, 97, 98, 99, 100, 101, 102, 104, 105, 106, 110, 111, 112, 113. Abraham Ball: 89, 90, 91. John Carswell: 6, 7, 8. Connaissance des Arts, Paris: 31, 34. Fitzwilliam Museum, Cambridge: 51, 52, 53, 54, 55, 56, 57, 58. Gemeentesmuseum, The Hague: 38, 41. Giraudon, Paris: 2, 3. Hessisches Landes-museum, Darmstadt: 109. Oliver van Oss: 39. George Rainbird Ltd., London: 43. Rijksmuseum, Amsterdam: 42, 45, 59. Sotheby & Co., London: 103. Cyril Staal: 76. Stedjelik Museum, Amsterdam: 107, 108. Victoria and Albert Museum, London: 9, 12, 13, 14, 15, 16, 50, 64, 68, 73, 74, 75, 77, 78, 79, 80, 81, 82, 83. Josiah Wedgwood & Sons Ltd: 65, 66, 67, 69, 70, 71, 72. Wellcome Museum of Medical Science, London: 44.

Dish, by Bernard Palissy (1510–90), or follower. First half of the sixteenth century (Victoria and Albert Museum, London. Salting Bequest). This dish is of earthenware ›delled in high relief and decorated in a number of richly coloured lead glazes. For designs such as this, which incorporate the human figure, the French potter Palissy ned to contemporary sculptors of the school of Jean Goujon.

2

3

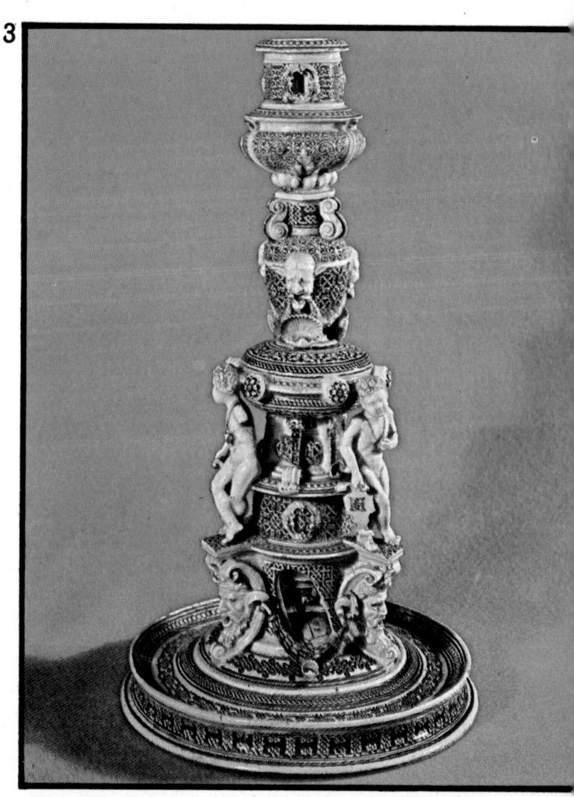

2 *Oval dish*, made in the studio of Bernard Palissy. Second half of the sixteenth century (Louvre, Paris). This earthenware dish with vivid-coloured mottled green, yellow, blue and purplish-brown lead glazes is decorated in low relief with the design known as '*La Fécondité*'. The elegantly elongated figure is in the style of the School of Fontainebleau and was later copied in London delftware.

3 *Table-candlestick*, Saint-Porchaire or *Henri Deux* ware. Sixteenth century (Petit Palais, Paris). The manufacture of fine ivory-coloured pottery, originally called *Henri Deux* ware, in Poitou, of which Saint-Porchaire is a locality, was of short duration, lasting from approximately 1530 to 1570. This piece, which was possibly made specifically for Henri II, is decorated with intricate traceries resembling those on contemporary bookbindings, in the renaissance style, and contrasting coloured slips, heightened by a few touches of stronger colours.

5

4 *Earthenware bottle moulded in relief and green glazed*, attributed to Isfahan. Seventeenth century (Victoria and Albert Museum, London). With the rise in Persia of a nationalist dynasty, the Safawids, at the beginning of the sixteenth century, there was a genuine renaissance in the field of ceramics. Five main types were produced: the so-called 'Kubachi' wares; Gombroon wares; late lustre-painted pottery; polychrome-painted wares; and monochrome and miscellaneous wares, to which category this bottle belongs. Monochrome-glazed vessels such as this were manufactured from the sixteenth to the eighteenth centuries and owe their origins to Chinese celadon, though the glazes have many different colours.

5 *Persian lustreware bottle*. Seventeenth century (Christie, Manson and Woods, London). The employment of the lustre technique ceased in Iran at the end of the fourteenth century and was not reintroduced until the second half of the seventeenth century. In later examples such as this, the designs are painted in lustre on the white ground and the decoration is generally restricted to floral or plant design, or, occasionally, 'leaf-specimen' treatment as illustrated here.

6 *Hexagonal tiles painted in under-glaze blue*, from the mosque of Murad II in Edirne. Dating fro AD 1435. These blue-and-white painted tiles were probably made in the workshops of Isnik (ancier Nicaea), in Western Anatolia, the great pottery-making centre of this period. The plant motifs may hav been inspired by decorative motifs on Chinese blue-and-white porcelain.

7 *Isnik ewer painted in under-glaze blue.* Dated 1510 (Godman Collection, Horsham, Sussex). Th inscription on the base of this ewer, which reads 'This vessel is in commemoration of Abraham, servan of God, of Kütahya', is written in Armenian but the technical and decorative characteristics of this ewe have led scholars to believe that it is Isnik in origin.

8 *Isnik tiles,* in the Rustem Pasha Mosque, Istanbul. 1561. The Rustum Pasha Mosque is without doub one of the masterpieces of the great Ottoman building period in the second half of the sixteenth century These exquisite tiles were brought from Isnik on muleback to the coast of the Sea of Marmara, whenc they were shipped to Istanbul. Infinitely complex patterns fit into the allotted space with extraordinar accuracy and are painted with skill and verve.

9 *White earthenware dish painted in under-glaze colours*, Kubachi, north Persia. Early seventeenth century (Victoria and Albert Museum, London). The name 'Kubachi' is derived from a small town in Daghestan in the Caucasus, where most of this pottery was discovered. It is evident that these wares were not produced locally since Kubachi had no pottery tradition; as the inhabitants were excellent metalworkers, it is possible that they traded their weapons for pottery.

10 *The base of a qalian, or hookah,* from Meshhed. First half of the seventeenth century (Christie, Manson and Woods, London). A *qalian* is of Eastern origin; a smoking-pipe with a long, flexible tube, the smoke is drawn through water which is retained in the base. The tube is attached to the side hole and the tall stem holds the tobacco cup fixed on top. This *qalian* base is decorated with panels enclosing animals and a relatively restricted vocabulary of animal forms.

11 *Beaker with turquoise glaze.* Late seventeenth century (Victoria and Albert Museum, London). This beaker, the colour of which is opaque and very well preserved, was almost certainly designed to hold toilet accessories.

11

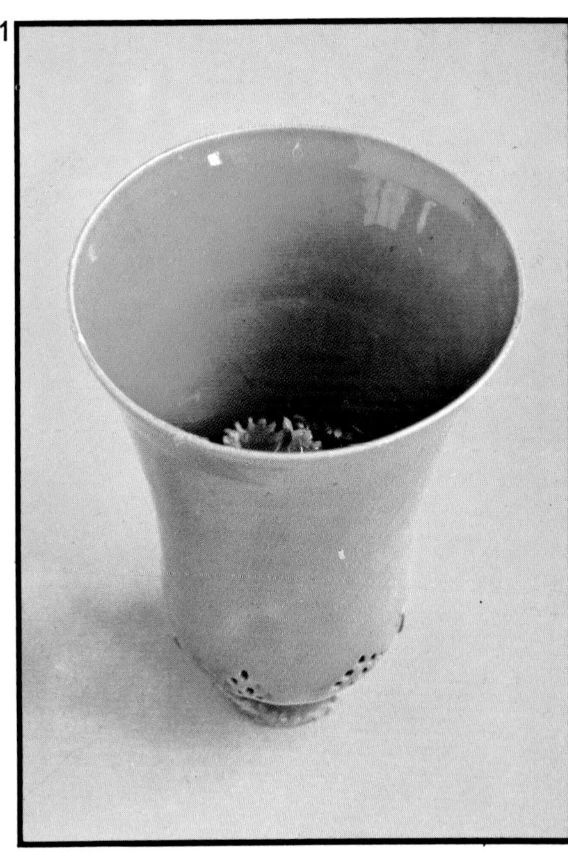

12 *Dish*, Seville. Fifteenth century (Victoria and Albert Museum, London). This colourful dish decorated with a mythical animal is glazed by the *cuerda seca* (dry-cord) method. This type of glazing was first used in the Near East but had been practised by the potters of Cordoba since the eleventh century. A mixture of manganese and grease was used to paint the outline on the body and these lines served as barriers to prevent the colours from running during the glaze-firing. Wares decorated by this method are often clumsily potted but tend to show imaginative and vigorous designs.

13 *Bowl*, Manises. Early fifteenth century (Victoria and Albert Museum, London). The decoration on this bowl is painted in brown-gold lustre and a blue stripe encircles the rim. The decoration shows a Portuguese ship sailing over four dolphins. The tree of life designs on the exterior are based on earlier Andalusian motifs, while the shape of the bowl with its straight, sloping surface is related to prototypes made at Malaga.

14 *Plate painted in lustre and blue*. *c*.1428 (Wallace Collection, London). This plate bears the arms of Philip the Good (1396–1467), Duke of Burgundy, who married Isabella of Portugal in about 1429.

13

12

14

15 *Ewer, or aquamanile*, Manises. Early sixteenth century (Victoria and Albert Museum, London). This ewer, which was used for pouring water over the hands between courses at table, was made at Manises near Valencia. Painted in lustre, the heraldic lion with which it is decorated is associated with the lords of Paterna of the House of Aragon-Segorbe.

16 *Dish*, Manises. *c.*1469–79 (Victoria and Albert Museum, London). This dish in applied relief and painted in lustre and blue, is decorated with the arms of Isabella of Castille and Ferdinand, King of Sicily, who were married in 1469.

17 *Dish*, Catalonia. Early seventeenth century (Victoria and Albert Museum, London). This dish painted in blue on a lustre patterned background is highly characteristic of Catalan pottery. Lustre pottery began to be made in Catalonia and Aragon towards the end of the fifteenth century, or early in the sixteenth century, in imitation of Manises ware. Slightly different designs, and the quality and colour of the glazes and body-materials, help to identify them from Valencia lustre.

6

17

18 *Dish*, Talavera. Seventeenth century (Victoria and Albert Museum, London). Decorated with the helmeted head and shoulders of a man, this dish is characteristic of the almost wholly figurative designs produced at Talavera de la Reina which ranged from realistically detailed scenes to powerful, sketchy caricatures as illustrated here. The great pottery centre of Talavera, which became increasingly important as lustreware lost its prominence, was some eighty miles south west of Madrid. It reached the peak of its excellence and earned worldwide recognition in the seventeenth century, encouraged in part by a decree of Philip III which ordered that all silver table-services and church plate be inventoried, restricted or even confiscated, hence encouraging the wider use of pottery among the ruling classes. The basic material used by Talavera potters was a finely textured clay which fired to a light tan. An opaque tin glaze provided the ground for their painted decorations in blue, yellow, green and orange.

19 *Tea-caddy*, Alcora. Mid-eighteenth century (Victoria and Albert Museum, London). This tea-caddy moulded in the form of silverware was made at the small town of Alcora, near Castellón de la Plana. Artists from France were brought to Alcora by the patron of the factory, the Count of Aranda, to teach his potters how to decorate their wares in the accepted idiom of the day. This tea-caddy which is decorated with designs reminiscent of the delicate arabesques of Jean Bérain, contemporary engravings and rococo floral motifs is typical of their style.

20 *Maiolica plate*, Cafaggiolo. *c.*1520 (Victoria and Albert Musum, London). Depicting a maiolica artist decorating the rim of a plate in front of two patrons whose portraits he will later paint in the well, the decoration of this plate extends over the whole area with a background of dark blue brushstrokes which is a characteristic stylistic treatment of wares produced in this area. It is attributed to a painter who signed himself 'Jacopo'.

21 *Albarello*, attributed to Siena. *c.*1500 (Victoria and Albert Musum, London). *Albarelli*, which were generally tall jars with nipped-in waists, were used by apothecaries to hold dry drugs and medicaments. Maiolica was first made in Siena at the end of the fifteenth century under the influence of Faenza.

22 *Oval dish with moulded rims painted in polychrome*, Urbino. *c.*1560–70 (Victoria and Albert Museum, London). The centre of this dish, which is painted in the fashionable decorative style, depicts 'The Gathering of the Manna'. From the workshop of Orazio Fontana, the sophisticated designs follow those originated by the School of Raphael in the *Loggie* of the Vatican.

18

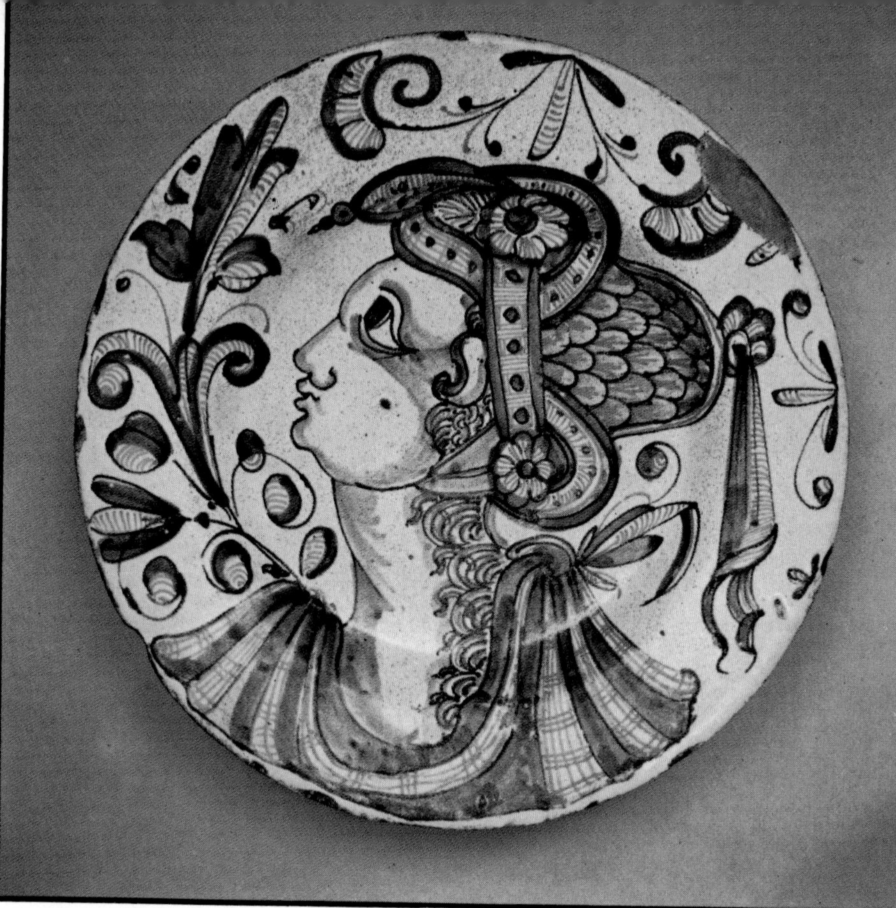

19

21

22

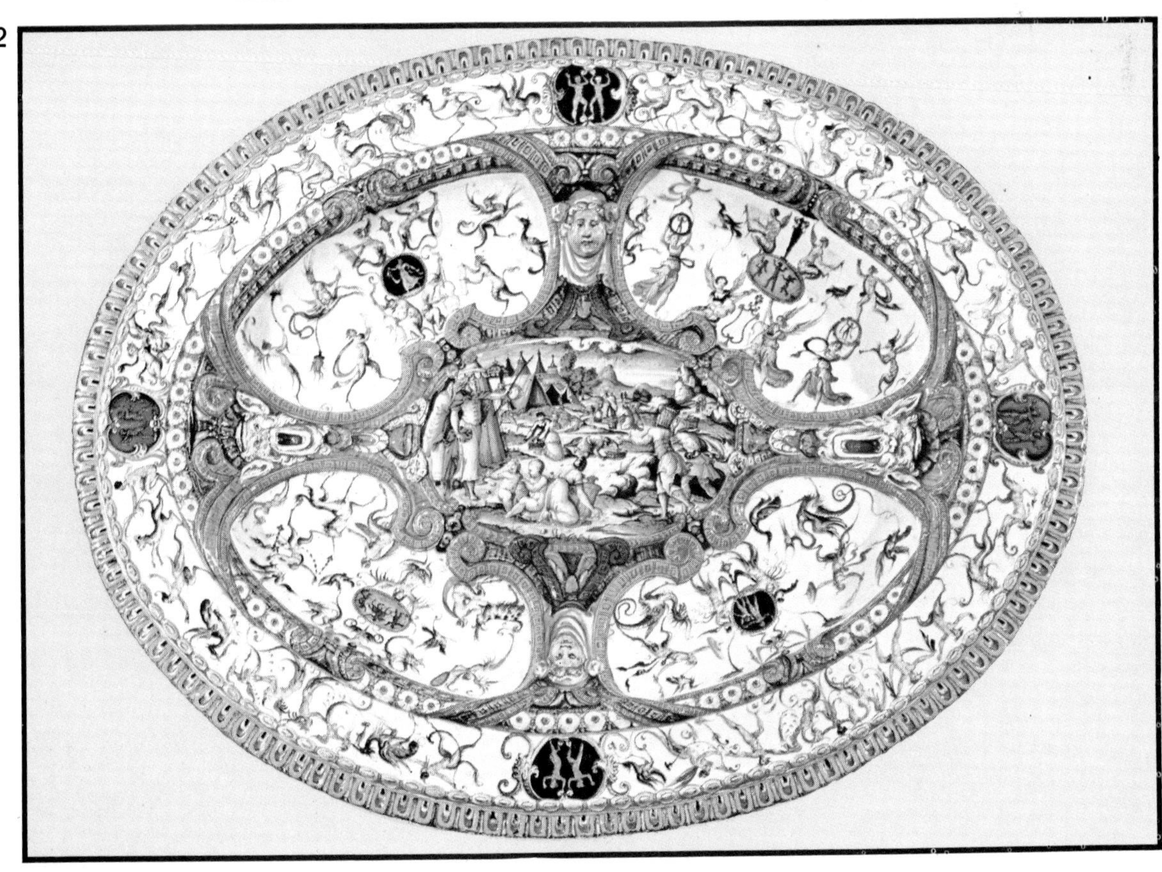

23 *Dish*, Faenza. *c.*1530 (Victoria and Albert Museum, London). This dish, which shows gadrooning in imitation of metalwork, was made at a time when decoration gradually took less and less account of the shape or use of a vessel.

24 *Plate painted by Nicola Pellipario*, Castel Durante. *c.*1519 (Fitzwilliam Museum, Cambridge). The heraldic shield within a *bianco-sopra-bianco* (decoration in white glaze-mixture) border of palmettes identifies this service made for Isabella d'Este, with her favourite devices, by Nicola Pellipario, the greatest Urbino master of the *istoriato* style. The scene around the border depicts the story of Peleus and Thetis.

25 *Dish signed by Maestro Giorgio Andreoli of Gubbio.* Dated 1527 in lustre on the back (Victoria and Albert Museum, London). The centre of this dish is decorated with the arms of Vitelli. The glowing ruby-red is produced by the use of copper and is characteristic of pottery from Gubbio.

23

24

25

Vase and cover, Deruta. *c.*1515 (Victoria and Albert Musum, London). This shape is characteristic ɔeruta ware which is generally decorated in either lustre or polychrome.

Salt-cellar. *c.*1580–1600 (Victoria and Albert Museum, London). It is likely that this salt-cellar was ·de as a commemorative piece since the bust of a soldier is painted in the well and the inscription ɜrs to his military prowess.

Inkstand, Urbino. *c.*1550–60 (Victoria and Albert Museum, London). The colouring, styles and ·delling of Faenza were brought to Urbino early in the sixteenth century.

27

28

30

29

31

29 *Vase*, Nevers. Early eighteenth century (Victoria and Albert Museum, London). Faience was introduced to Nevers by the Duke Luigi Gonzaga of Mantua, who became Duke of Nivernais in 1565 through his marriage to Henrietta of Cleves. The influence of Faenza and the Urbino pictorial style was strongly evident throughout its history. The scene on this vase depicts the return of the prodigal son.

30 *Dish by Antoine Sigalon*, Nîmes. *c.*1580 (Victoria and Albert Museum, London). The reputation of the Huguenot potter, Antoine Sigalon, stems from such elaborately painted pieces as this.

31 *The underside of an oval dish*, Nevers, 1589 (Louvre, Paris). The decoration on the inside of this dish is reminiscent of late Urbino maiolica. The blue decoration became a speciality of Nevers faience.

32 *Ewer*, Rouen. *c.*1680 (Victoria and Albert Museum, London). A typical helmet shape, this ewer is of the type known as *'Violette'* faience, that is, faience painted in blue and other colours after the manner of Delft. Its polygonal shape and very precise decorative style are derived from the East.

33 *Wig-stand in blue-and-white*, Nevers. Late seventeenth century (Victoria and Albert Museum, London). In the course of time, pseudo-Oriental designs succeeded the Italian idiom at Nevers, as demonstrated by this wig-stand.

35

34

34 *Vase and cover*, Rouen. Late seventeenth century (Louvre, Paris). Painted in polychrome, this vase has an architectural quality reminiscent of the urns which decorated classical monuments.

35 *Sugar-castor*, Rouen. Early eighteenth century (Victoria and Albert Museum, London). Painted in blue-and-white, this attractive sugar-castor is another example of *Violette* faience.

37

36 *Drug-pot*, South Netherlands (Antwerp). *c.*1570 (Victoria and Albert Museum, London). This tin-glazed earthenware drug-pot painted in polychrome represents the type intended for the storage and dispensing of fluid medicaments, while the unspouted *albarello* was used for ointments and dry medicines.

37 *Dish*, Dutch. Late sixteenth or early seventeenth century (Victoria and Albert Museum, London). Depicting the infant St. John, this dish decorated with ochre arabesques and foliage around a central medallion is in the Italian Urbinesque tradition.

38 *Dish*, Dutch. Early seventeenth century (Gemeentemuseum, The Hague). The simple but strong design of this early plate was superseded in later Du pottery by more elaborate and frequently figurative designs.

39 *Tiles*. Six decorative tiles ranging from Flemish in the late sixteenth century, through to Dutch in the late seventeenth century. (Private Collection.)

40 *Dish*, Dutch. Early seventeenth century (Gemeentemuseum, The Hague). Decorated with blue and ochre bands and a blue-dash border, the central des of this dish is based on a Venetian pattern. The thick, sloping strokes of blue on the border which gave rise to the description 'blue-dash' were prompted either coiled rope or some metalworker's ornamentation.

41 *Dish*, Dutch. Early seventeenth century (Victoria and Albert Museum, London). The entire surface of this plate is enamelled opaque blue. It is thought have been made in Rotterdam.

42 *Drug-pot decorated with the arms of Haarlem and Amsterdam*. 1610 (Rijksmuseum, Amsterdam). Small cylindrical drug-pots such as this have in the p often been dug up in London as well as in Holland and are usually simply decorated with rings of blue, manganese and yellow.

38

39

41

43

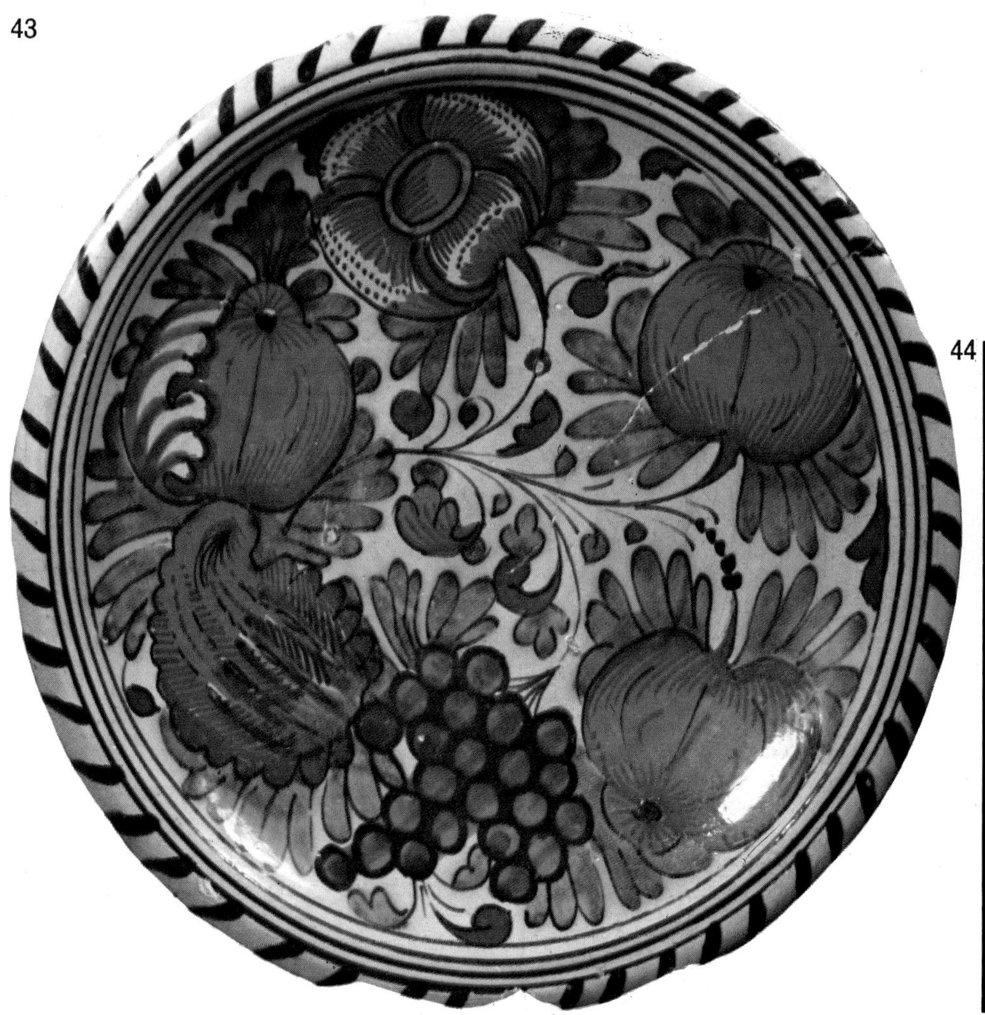

44

45

43 *Dish*, Dutch. Early seventeenth century (Fitzwilliam Museum, Cambridge). The strong, almost crude, colours of this dish and the composition, which is slightly provincial in character, are typical of many Dutch wares produced at this time. The blue-dash border was later adopted at Lambeth, and Bristol in the blue-dash chargers.

44 *Apothecary jar with peacock design*, Dutch (Wellcome Museum of Medical Science, London). The design of two peacocks facing a basket of fruit or flowers was introduced sometime before 1665 and remained a popular motif for the next hundred years. Although large numbers of these peacock-jars were made, nearly all were unmarked, making attribution to any particular factory difficult.

45 *Tile in blue-and-white* after the official architect to the Dutch Court, Daniel Marot. Dutch. Seventeenth century (Rijksmuseum, Amsterdam). Tiles were made in sets of four with an integrated corner-pattern, but in the early seventeenth century this degenerated into a flower or a shape unrelated to the central motif, while at the same time blue-and-white became more popular, superseding the earlier pomegranate and grape polychrome decoration.

47

46 *Wig-stand*, Dutch. Late seventeenth century (Victoria and Albert Museum, London). Blue-and-white, in imitation of Chinese porcelain, this Delft wig-stand is decorated with an Oriental scene which strives to reproduce the original as closely as possible.

47 *Tea-caddy*, Dutch, *c.*1700 (Victoria and Albert Museum, London). This tea-caddy which follows a traditional silver shape is painted in black enamel in imitation of Chinese lacquer.

48 *Milk-pan*, Dutch. 1690-94 (Victoria and Albert Museum, London). Probably from the set made for the dairy at Hampton Court, this milk-pan has a pouring lip to facilitate the cream separating process. Delft pottery was very fashionable in England and, rather than relying on English imitations, popular demand encouraged its importation in large quantities from Holland.

49

49 *Tile after Daniel Marot, in the manner of Delft.* Seventeenth century (Rijksmuseum, Amsterdam). The tile output in Holland was enormous and tile-making remained a major export industry for more than two hundred years. For example, in 1646 a floor of tiles is recorded as having been laid at Nantes necessitating a consignment of seven thousand tiles in sixteen crates.

50 *Posset-pot*, possibly Lambeth. 1696 (Victoria and Albert Museum, London). This attractive pot was intended for hot spiced and herbal drinks, sucked out through a spout at the front which had strainer holes at its base on the inside. The blue decoration is derived from Chinese porcelain of the Wan-li period (1573–1619) with which English and Dutch potters had been familiar since late in the sixteenth century.

51

52

53

51 *Blue-dash charger*, English. 1637 (Fitzwilliam Museum, Cambridge. Glaisher Collection). English delftware dishes and chargers such as this, have survived in great quantity and commonly depict biblical subjects or portraits of royalty and popular heroes.

52 *Blue-dash charger*, English. 1640 (Fitzwilliam Museum, Cambridge. Glaisher Collection). Adam and Eve shown beneath an apple tree around which is coiled the serpent, was a biblical subject commonly employed by decorators of blue-dash chargers. It is always difficult to be certain which of these chargers were made in London and which in Bristol and Brislington, where delftware was certainly being made from early in the 1640s. The foliage in the Bristol versions tends to be heavily sponged rather than drawn, and one may suspect that the cruder Adam and Eve plates, showing less familiarity with engraved sources, were not made in London.

53 *Jug*, English. Second half of the seventeenth century (Fitzwilliam Museum, Cambridge. Glaisher Collection). This jug is decorated in the manner of late Ming porcelain, a style, with its typical motifs such as tall plants, sketchy landscapes and stylized figures, much favoured by the Lambeth potters. In Holland such pieces of Dutch manufacture are known as 'Hollands Porcelyn', and are often deceptively like the porcelain originals, but English pieces in this style are seldom of such high quality.

4

54 *Tankard, or Apostelenkrüge*, Kreussen. First half of the seventeenth century (Fitzwilliam Museum, Cambridge. Glaisher Collection). A distinctive light brown-grey stoneware was manufactured at Kreussen, near Bayreuth in Bavaria, which was invariably given a coating of colours. A strong resemblance between the decoration on Kreussen stoneware and on contemporary Bohemian glass, which was painted with enamels of the same kind, suggests that the same artists decorated both. The jugs, flasks and tankards manufactured at Kreussen were decorated with stock patterns such as *Apostolenkrüge* (the figures of the Apostles), as depicted on this tankard.

55 *Tankard*, Westerwald. 1700 (Fitzwilliam Museum, Cambridge. Glaisher Collection). The Westerwald district, which became known as 'The Land of Pot-bakers' because of the enormous number of factories in the area, lies on the Rhine, opposite Koblenz. This grey stoneware tankard is decorated in blue and manganese.

56 *Wine-bottle or 'Bellarmine'*, made either in Cologne or Frechen. Second half of the sixteenth century (Fitzwilliam Museum, Cambridge. Glaisher Collection). 'Bellarmines', known also as 'Greybeards', '*Barmannskrügen*' or '*Barbmans*', acquired the name by which they are best known in England because of their supposed caricature-likeness to the Italian Catholic divine, Cardinal Roberto Bellarmino (1542–1621), whose publications incited anger among Protestants. This characteristic 'Bellarmine' with its bearded mask on a short neck is decorated with five star-like medallions enclosing the heads of Roman soldiers.

56

57

58

57 *Jug*, Bunzlau. Mid-eighteenth century (Fitzwilliam Museum, Cambridge. Glaisher Collection). Th pottery at Bunzlau, in the province of Silesia, now part of Poland, produced stoneware from the eighteent century. The grey body was disguised by a coating of coffee- or rust-coloured glaze and was often decorate with applied reliefs as demonstrated by this jug which carries reliefs of flowers and leaves and a Prussia eagle bearing the cypher of Frederick the Great.

58 *Inkstand*, Westerwald. *c.*1730 (Fitzwilliam Museum, Cambridge. Glaisher Collection). This rath elaborate and fanciful inkstand is typical of the later wares produced at Westerwald. Birds and anima were similarly rendered and standing figures of men holding small pots, probably intended for use as sal cellars, have been recorded.

59 *Teapot and cup and saucer*, German. 1710–15 (Victoria and Albert Museum, London). The designs c these pieces in polished stoneware derive directly from silver models. They also recall vessels cut fror hardstones, their glittering surfaces having understandably been confused.

60 *Teapot*, German. *c.*1710–13 (Victoria and Albert Museum, London). This stoneware teapot, with cu and polished details, which is attributable to Böttger, shows the influence not only of Chinese models bu also of the court silversmith Johann Irminger who was attached to the Dresden factory from 1710 until afte 1720. The enamelling of the flower reliefs has been executed with great skill and is possibly by the Dresde artist, J. T. Meyer.

61 *Two teapots or coffee-pots*, German. Left: *c.*1710–20. Right: *c.*1712–15 (Victoria and Albert Museum London). Böttger in 1710 perfected a shining black glaze (from cobalt and manganese) which is illustrated b the pot on the right; it has been painted with unfired gold, silver and colours in the style of Oriental lacquer The pot on the left is partly polished and decorated with silver mounts.

61

63

62

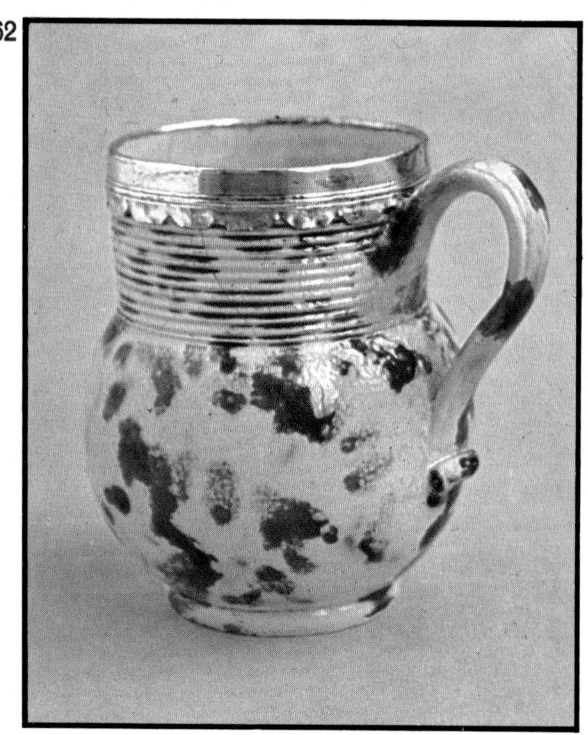

Mug from Dwight's Pottery at Fulham. Late seventeenth century (Victoria and Albert Museum, London). Of white stoneware in ilver mount, this mug is decorated with splashes of colour. It was said by a near-contemporary of Dwight that 'he hath brought it oneware) to greater perfection than it has attained where it hath been used for many ages, insomuch that the Company of Glass-llers of London, who are dealers for that commodity, have contracted with the inventor to buy only of his English manufacture d refuse the foreign'.

Bottle made at the Fulham Pottery by Dwight. Late seventeenth century (Victoria and Albert Museum, London). In 1672, John vight was granted a patent for the manufacture of 'transparent earthenware' and 'stoneware vulgarly called Cologne ware', the mmercial success of the Fulham Pottery being founded above all on the latter. This bottle is made of brown stoneware and corated with applied motifs such as birds and snails in white slip.

Teapot, English. Late seventeenth or early eighteenth century (Victoria and Albert Museum, London). This red stoneware apot decorated with gilding and *chinoiserie* decoration shows the influence of the Elers brothers, who were thought to have come om Holland in the wake of William of Orange. Any piece of fine quality, English, seventeenth-century red stoneware that cannot associated with Dwight, may be considered as probably made by the Elers.

65 *'Cauliflower ware' teapot, Wedgwood.* Late 1750s (Josiah Wedgwood and Sons Limited, Barlaston, Staffordshire). Towards the latter part of Wedgwood's partnership with Thomas Whieldon, from 1754 to 1759, he produced a deep green glaze which was a complete novelty for use on earthenware. Such a colour suggested foliage, and it was soon possible to imitate in earthenware the amusing cauliflowers and other vegetables which had previously been made only by the porcelain factories.

66 *Black basaltes vase in the 'Etruscan' style,* Wedgwood and Bentley. Early 1770s (Josiah Wedgwood and Sons Limited, Barlaston, Staffordshire). The British Ambassador at the Court of Naples, Sir William Hamilton, owned a fine collection of the pottery vases which were being discovered at that time in Etruscan tombs. These were illustrated in detail in volumes of plates which Wedgwood and Bentley acquired and, seeing the possibilities in copying them, they soon made a name for their 'Etruscan' vases.

67 *Coffee-pot in 'Queen's ware',* Wedgwood. Late eighteenth century (Josiah Wedgwood and Sons Limited, Barlaston, Staffordshire). Though other factories, in particular the Leeds pottery, made very fine cream-coloured earthenware, it was Wedgwood's own perfected variety of it, which Queen Charlotte allowed him to call 'Queen's ware', that was to prove the foundation of his fortunes. The transfer-printed decoration on this coffee-pot was carried out by Sadler and Green of Liverpool.

68 *Dinner-plate painted in enamels from the dinner-service of Catherine the Great,* Wedgwood. *c.*1773–74 (Victoria and Albert Museum, London). In 1773 the Empress Catherine of Russia ordered from Wedgwood a magnificent dinner- and dessert-service, including every sort of tureen, sauce-boat and dish as well as these plates; nine hundred and fifty-two pieces in all. Each piece was decorated with an interesting view of an English house, garden or other scene, in this case a folly with a view of Wakefield in the background. Wedgwood's profit on this undertaking may have been as little as £100 but the reputation it gained for him both in England and overseas was more than enough to compensate.

69

70

72

Teaset in jasper ware, Wedgwood. Early 1780s (Josiah Wedgwood and is Limited, Barlaston, Staffordshire). Following the Adam precedent, dgwood used a coloured fine-grained stoneware (called 'jasper') for the :kground and ornamented it with white classical figures in relief. The :oration on this teaset represents 'Domestic Employment' and was designed Lady Templetown; the pieces were modelled by William Hackwood.

Plaque in jasper ware of the Dancing Hours, Wedgwood. Late 1770s siah Wedgwood and Sons Limited, Barlaston, Staffordshire). Modelled by nn Flaxman. Plaques such as this, were made for insertion into wood or rble chimney-pieces. A number of these chimney-pieces have survived but fewer than the number of surviving plaques would suggest, partly because torian collectors liked to display the plaques in their cabinets and mercilessly oke up their fireplaces to get at them.

Black basaltes ware, Wedgwood, Etruria. Late eighteenth century (Josiah edgwood and Sons Limited, Barlaston, Staffordshire). Wedgwood evolved s dense black stoneware, which was much more vitrified than earthenware, as suitable ceramic body for his Etruscan vases. He called it 'basaltes' thinking it it looked like basaltic rock, and boasted that 'the black is sterling and will t for ever'. The vase on the right is emblematic of water.

Soup-tureen in 'Queen's Ware', Wedgwood. Late eighteenth century osiah Wedgwood and Sons Limited, Barlaston, Staffordshire). Based on a ntemporary silver shape, this design is illustrated in the catalogue of 'Useful ares', 1774. Even in domestic wares where convenience was essential, edgwood's pieces retain the elegance of form characteristic of Adam taste.

73

74

3 *Toby Jug* made at Ralph Wood's factory, Burslem. *c.*1780 (Victoria and Albert Museum, London). White earthenware decorated with coloured lead glazes, marked: 1/Ra Wood Burslem', impressed. The idea for the ever-popular 'Toby Jug' is attributed to Ralph Wood although other examples of jugs moulded in human form can be aced back to ancient times. It is suggested that Wood's version was based upon a well-known toper of the day, Harry Elwes, who was pictured on an engraved ballad-sheet f 1761 as Toby Fillpot. Many varieties of such jugs are attributed to Ralph Wood and his son of the same name (1748–95), but it is known that such other skilled potters s Hollins, Neale, Lakin and Poole, Pratt, Walton, Davenport and Spode all made similar wares.

4 *'The Vicar and Moses'* attributed to Aaron Wood, made by Ralph Wood's factory, Burslem. *c.*1770 (Victoria and Albert Museum, London). White earthenware with oloured lead glazes, marked 'Ra. Wood/Burslem/62', impressed. *The Vicar and Moses* pulpit group belongs to the finely modelled Wood figures which are thought to be e work of Aaron Wood, the younger brother of the elder Ralph. The origin of the subject is vague but was obviously based on the reputation of a local vicar who was o often drunk that his clerk Moses had to read the lesson for him. This model appears in the long list of earlier figures that were made by the firm of William Kent Limited f Burslem up until 1962. Usually the later versions lack the cherubs and draperies on the pulpit and are badly painted.

5 *Equestrian group called 'Hudibras'* made at Ralph Wood's factory, Burslem. *c.*1770–80 (Victoria and Albert Museum, London). Earthenware with coloured glaze, arked with an impressed '41'. Mounted on his pathetic nag, the figure of Sir Hudibras is derived from an engraving by William Hogarth which was designed for an lustrated edition of Samuel Butler's poem, published in 1726. The Woods were one of the few families of Staffordshire potters who occasionally marked their wares with n impressed factory mark, thus many examples, though unmarked, can be safely attributed to them since they were produced from the same moulds as the marked pieces.

6 *Soup-plate*, Wedgwood. Early nineteenth century (Private Collection). Transfer-printed with a design of a Chinese vase standing on a table surrounded by flowers nd bamboos, the decoration on this plate is likely to be that referred to in surviving letters of late 1805 and early 1806 which describe the firm as embarking on services ecorated with 'the Chinese figure in the centre' and also, the 'New Chinese pattern with Urn'. The Wedgwood firm's first blue-printed wares came on the market in about 805, when Spode and Minton were both engaged in meeting this new demand. Josiah Wedgwood Senior died in 1795 and had, it was later reported, stoutly refused to ake any such ware because of solicitation from his painters, who feared it would result in their dismissal. It was when his son Josiah II became head of the pottery that change took place, and it was realized that they must cater for the prevailing fashion or lose a considerable amount of worthwhile business.

77 

78 

77 *Falstaff*, marked 'Wood and Caldwell'. *c.*1810 (Victoria and Albert Museum, London). In 1790 Enoch Wood took James Caldwell into a partnership that was to contin until 1818, their impressed mark over these years being 'Wood and Caldwell'. The figure of Falstaff is typical of the approach to earthenware figures by many manufacture during the first decades of the nineteenth century. Their aim was to make available, at the sort of prices paid at fairs or markets, good imitations of the more expensive, earli porcelain.

78 *The Reverend George Whitefield by Enoch Wood*, Burslem. Early nineteenth century (Victoria and Albert Museum, London). Among the most famous of Enoch Wooc busts are those of John Wesley, which he first modelled from life in 1781. The Reverend George Whitefield follows the same tradition, although lacking the impressiveness the early Wesley. The earthenware bust is painted in enamel colours.

81

79 *Jug*, probably Staffordshire. *c.*1810–15 (Victoria and Albert Museum, London). Platinum was used to acquire a lustrous silver effect in various styles, of which the heavy pottery reproduction of silver and plate is the least successful. Lighter and more pleasing effects were achieved by the process used here which is described as 'resist lustring'.

80 *Cup and saucer*, probably New Hall, Staffordshire. *c.*1815 (Victoria and Albert Museum, London). This cup and saucer made of bone china and decorated with enamel colours and pink lustre is of a type usually attributed to the New Hall factory which ceased production in 1835.

81 *Jug*, Staffordshire. *c.*1815 (Victoria and Albert Museum, London). This jug, the silver designs of which appear to have been applied by hand on to a previously fired canary-yellow enamel ground, represents what is probably the most sought-after type of lustreware. Jugs more commonly than any other item were produced in this colour, although mugs, vases, plates and figures are known.

83

82

82 *Jug, signed 'J. Phillips Hylton Pottery'.* Sunderland. *c.*1820 (Victoria and Albert Museum, London). Sunderland is probably the best known pottery centre associated with early nineteenth-century lustreware. Many of the wares produced by the six major companies in the area were marked; thus attribution is often easier than with Staffordshire ware. This pink lustre jug decorated with enamel colours and a transfer-print from an engraving of the Iron Bridge over the River Wear, bears a verse on its reverse side, and was presumably made as a commemorative piece for a sailor to give to his loved one.

83 *Watch-stand,* Sunderland. *c.*1820–26 (Victoria and Albert Museum, London). Decorated in pink lustre and enamel colours, this watch-stand was made by the firm Dixon, Austin and Company, whose popular wares included the representation of such figures as Joan of Arc, Napoleon and the Duke of Wellington. It is interesting to note that this factory also produced carpet-bowls which are normally only associated with Scottish factories.

84 *Jules Perrot as Gringoire and Carlotta Grisi as Esmeralda from the ballet La Esmeralda* shown at Her Majesty's Theatre, 9 March, 1844, Staffordshire. *c.*1845 (Oliver Sutton Antiques, London). This type of Staffordshire figure first appeared in the 1820s. Made from plaster-of-Paris moulds the Victorian potter showed great ingenuity in producing an apparently complicated figure from quite simple moulds. As workers were swept into the town by the late tide of the Industrial Revolution, the demand for entertainment grew, and, as demonstrated by these figures, it was to the world of entertainment that the Staffordshire potters turned for their inspiration.

85 *Two figures of Napoleon.* Heights 24 ins and 2¾ ins. Staffordshire, *c.*1845 (Oliver Sutton Antiques, London). More Staffordshire figures of Napoleon I were produced than of any other single personality. It is possible that some of them were intended for export to the French market but there is no conclusive evidence to support this theory. It is likely that the large demand from the English market may have been partly created by the many theatrical representations of Napoleon's campaigns.

86 *Two figures of Garibaldi* by Thomas Parr, Staffordshire. *c.*1861 (Oliver Sutton Antiques, London). Both these figures of the great Italian revolutionary, Garibaldi, were based on a print in a supplement to the 'Illustrated London News' dated 26 January, 1861. Their maker, Thomas Parr, modelled fine, complex figures in the round well into the flat-back period.

87 *Watch-holder,* Staffordshire. *c.*1850 (Oliver Sutton Antiques, London). This watch-holder illustrates the legend in which Llewelyn, Prince of North Wales, slew his faithful hound, Gelert, mistakenly thinking the dog had attacked and killed his son and heir.

88 *Little Red Riding Hood*, Staffordshire. *c.*1848 (Oliver Sutton Antiques, London). One of a rare pair depicting this popular children's story.

91

89 *Wellington in a Cocked Hat*, English. (Private Collection.) With the perfection, during the 1840s, of the technique of transfer-printing in colour on ceramics, lids for the containers of cosmetic preparations and foods became cheap and popular decorative objects. This is one of the many pot-lids bearing portraits of well-known figures.

90 *The Bay of Naples*, English. (Private Collection.) Just as Victorian ladies used attractive containers for their cosmetics, so also did the gentlemen. This decorative lid was made for a pot of Naples Shaving Paste.

91 *Alexandra Palace*, English. (Private Collection.) This originally shaped lid marks the Exhibition of 1873. Pot-lids were frequently used as a popular means of commemorating important people and events.

92

92 *Burmantofts faience.* c.1880–1904 (Private Collection). Burmantofts faience, first produced in 1880, was called after the suburb of Leeds where the pottery was situated. The double-gourd vase, rose-leaf bowl and bottle illustrated here are characteristic of the earthenware in coloured glazes produced at this factory.

93

93 *Vase and jug with flowing glazes* designed by Christopher Dresser, Linthorpe Pottery. c.1879–82 (Private Collection). Christopher Dresser, the designer of these two pieces of art-pottery, was the co-founder of the Linthorpe Pottery which was established just south of Middlesbrough in 1879.

94 *Earthenware vase with a flowing glaze* designed by Christopher Dresser, Ault Pottery. c.1895 (Private Collection). This vase is derived from a Japanese model; in the context of European ceramics of the 1890s its simple geometry was revolutionary.

95 *Vases*, with flowing glazes, Bretby Art Pottery. c.1885 (Private Collection). Henry Tooth left the Linthorpe Pottery where he was pottery manager to set up on his own at Woodville, near Burton-upon-Trent. The ware he produced here with great success was called 'Bretby Art Pottery'.

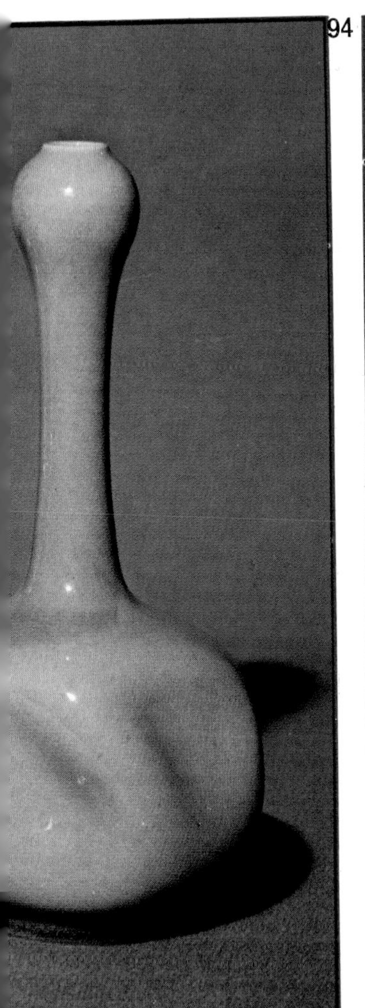

94

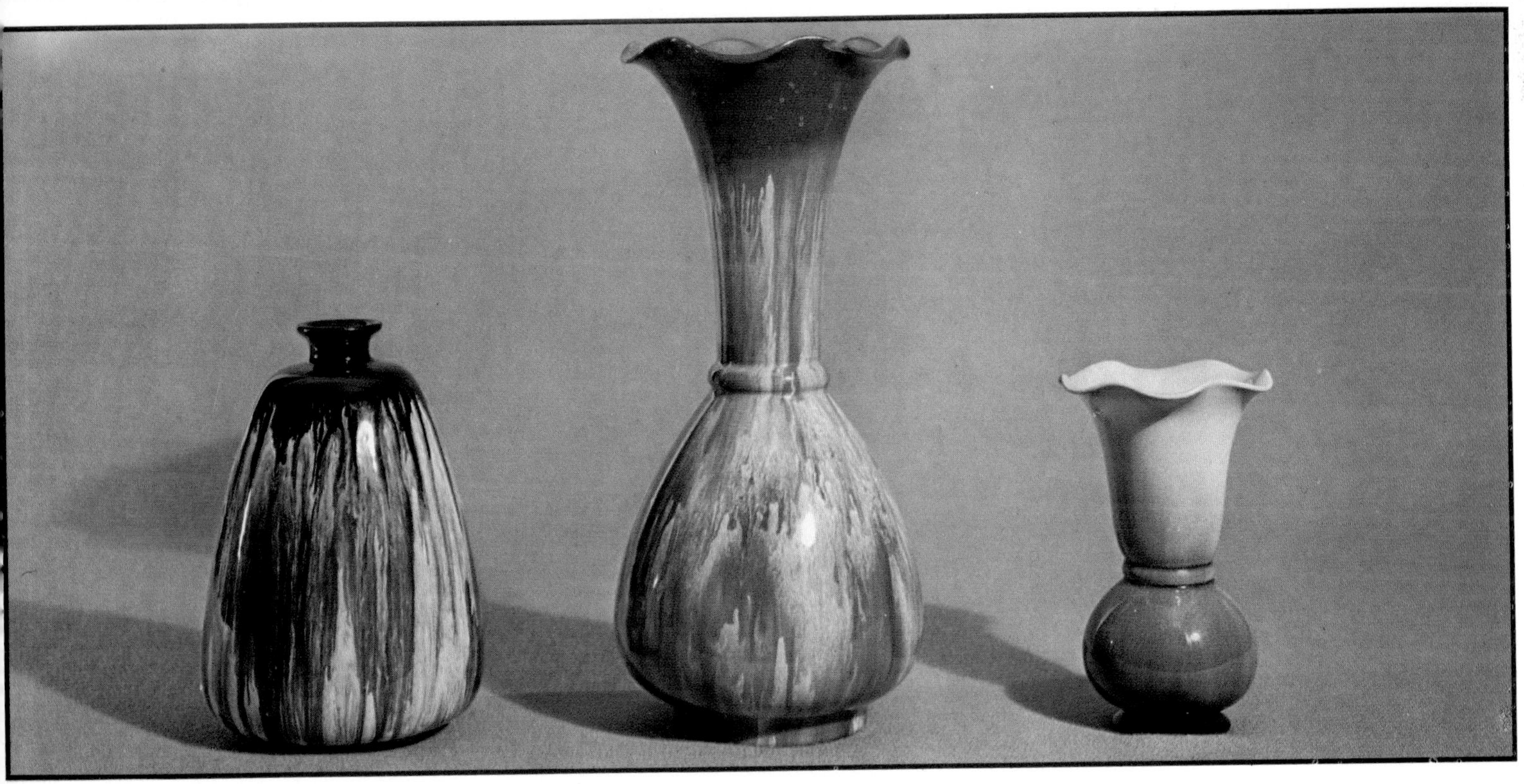

96 *Vase*, William de Morgan Pottery, Sand's End, Fulham, 1888–97 (Fulham Public Library, London). This lead-glazed earthenware vase which is decorated by Joe Jus with gold lustre and painted decoration shows both the influence of Islamic pottery and the enthusiasm of the Arts and Crafts Movement for naturalistic ornament.

97 *Two-handled vase in salt-glazed stoneware* by Martin Brothers, Southall. 1899 (Fulham Public Library, London). Martinware, to which the brothers Martin ga their name is rich in the variety of its shapes. Decoration is incised and coloured in a similar manner to that of Doulton stoneware decoration. Many of the pottery sha modelled by R. W. Martin show Oriental influence, as does the decoration of this piece, which was incised and coloured by Edwin Martin.

98 *Earthenware Vase with sgraffiato decoration through the slip* by C. H. Brannam, Barnstaple. 1888 (Private Collection). Called 'Barum ware' after the Roman name Barnstaple, Brannam's pottery was hand-thrown. This piece is signed with the initials W. B. for William Baron, the decorator. In 1899, Baron started his own pottery

99 *Carrara ware vase and Lambeth faience vase,* Doulton, Lambeth. Left: 1887–89. Right: 1889–91 (Doulton and Company Limited, London): As the success Doulton Ware grew, new types of art-pottery were added to the range. Different bodies were used as well as different types of decoration, represented here by enamel stoneware on the left and under-glaze decorated earthenware on the right.

100 *Lizards on a Rock and Vase,* Doulton, Lambeth early twentieth century (Doulton and Company Limited, London). Both these pieces are made of salt-glaz stoneware and decorated by Mark V. Marshall. Marshall began working for Doulton's in about 1876 after having been employed by Martin brothers.

96

98

97

101

102

101 *Vases* by Auguste Delaherche, rue Blomet, Paris. *c.*1890 (Bethnal Green Museum, London). These two stoneware vases, which illustrate the concern of Delaherche with the elaboration of glaze effects, also indicate the remarkable strength of form in his work. The career of this French artist-potter extended well into the twentieth century and passed through many different phases.

102 *Vases* by Adrien Dalpayrat (1844–1901), A. Debros et Cie, Bourg-la-Reine, near Paris (Bethnal Green Museum, London). The stoneware vase on the left was made in 1896 and decorated with a red glaze streaked with green and that on the right, *c.*1900 is decorated with a red glaze washed with blue-green. Dalpayrat's strong sense of form is perhaps seen at its best in these slightly asymmetrical shapes which he produced at the end of the century.

103

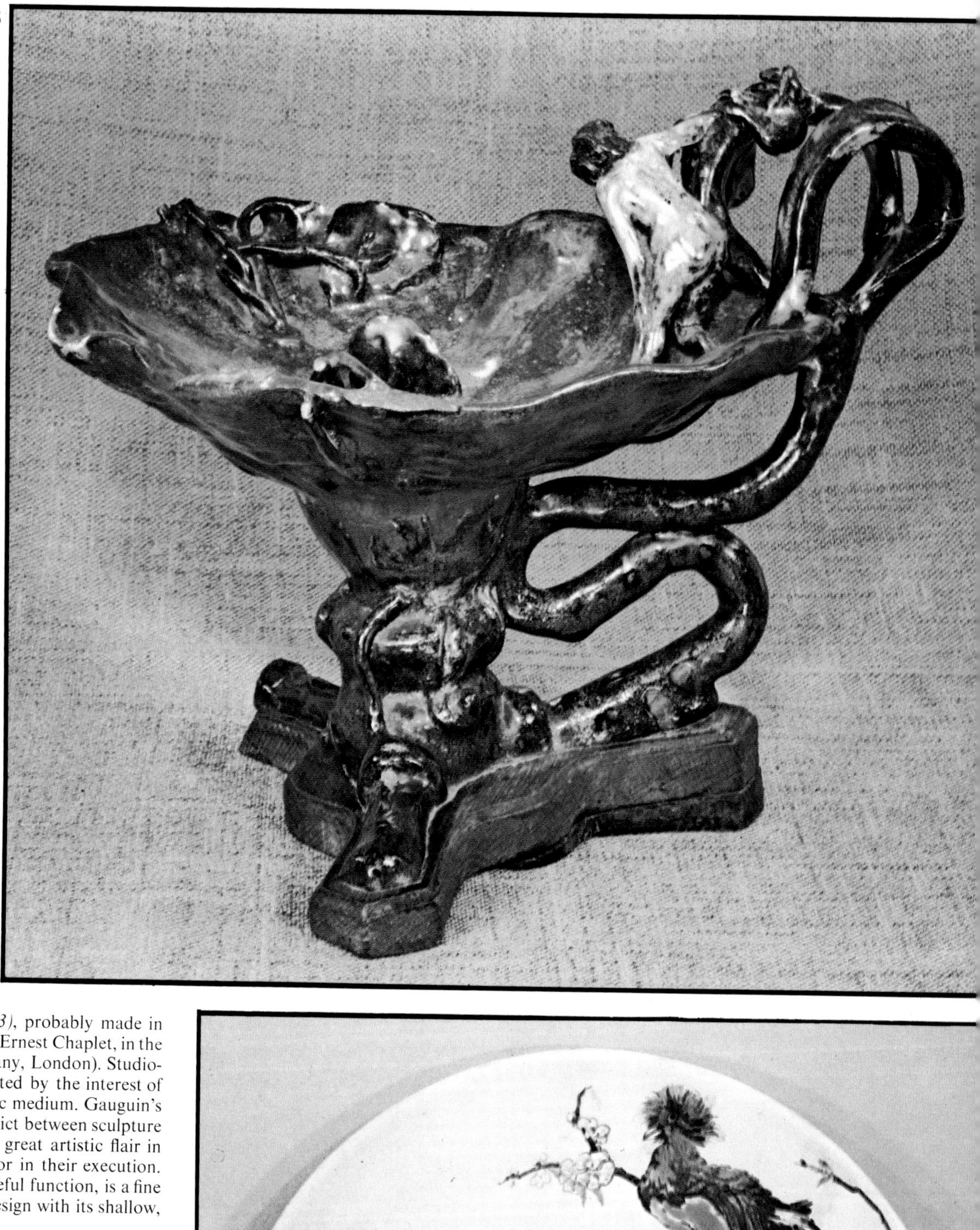

103 *Dish by Paul Gauguin (1848–1903)*, probably made in collaboration with the French ceramist, Ernest Chaplet, in the winter of 1887–88. (Sotheby and Company, London). Studio-pottery in France was profoundly affected by the interest of painters and other artists in the ceramic medium. Gauguin's work in this field displays a strong conflict between sculpture and ceramics; many of his pieces show great artistic flair in their conception but are technically poor in their execution. This important dish, while serving no useful function, is a fine example of naturalistic Art Nouveau design with its shallow, lily-strewn bowl and undulating handle.

104 *Dish by Theodore Deck (1823–91)*, the decoration designed and painted by Eléonore Escallier (1827–88), 1867 (Musée des Arts Décoratifs, Paris). Theodore Deck was the first of the artist-potters in the modern sense, setting himself up in Paris in 1856 to make decorative earthenware. The chief feature of his work is its remarkable variety, and perhaps for that reason he is now more clearly recognized for the range of his technical innovations than for his personal ceramic style. This earthenware dish decorated with an early example of painting in the revived Japanese style was shown at the Paris Exhibition of 1867. Mme. Escallier was one of many artists who painted on Deck's faience at about this time.

104

5 *Vase by Theodore Deck.* Late nineteenth century (Richard Dennis Antiques, London). Glazed with d-leaf insertion and impressed with the artist's monogram, this vase may belong to the last four years Deck's career, from 1887–1891, which he spent as art-director at Sèvres, the first practical potter ever reach that distinction.

6 *Rosewater-sprinkler by Theodore Deck. c.*1890 (Richard Dennis Antiques, London). This sprinkler, ade of glazed pottery with metal mounts, was designed for the Arab market and is clear evidence of the spiration that Deck gained from Near-Eastern and Persian wares.

106

107

108

7 *'The Deaf One' by Josef Mendes da Costa*, Dutch. *c.*1898 (Stedelijk Museum, Amsterdam). Belgian and Dutch Art Nouveau ceramics were inspired by ıences as diverse as Dutch delft, the English Arts and Crafts Movement, Javanese batiks and local folk traditions. In this stoneware group, Da Costa has ɜrted to rural simplicity and primitivism.

8 *Vase by Christian Johannes van der Hoef for the Amstelhoek Workshops*, Dutch. *c.*1900 (Stedelijk Museum, Amsterdam). The Amstelhoek Workshops were ·wn for their furniture and silver as well as their pottery. The decorations on their pottery were cut out with a knife and filled with clay of another colour in instance blue-and-white. The forms of the vases were known as 'amphorae', 'patherae' and 'cantharae' and their decoration was neo-Greek.

9 *Plate*, Rozenburg Plateelbakkerij, The Hague. *c.*1890 (Hessisches Landesmuseum, Darmstadt). The Rozenburg pottery which was founded at the Hague .885 was directed by Theodorus Colenbrander, an important figure in Dutch ceramics of this period. The design painted on this plate is inspired by Javanese iks and is in characteristic Rozenburg colours.

110 *Jar decorated by H. Wilcox* with lilies on a green ground, Rookwood. 1900 (Bethnal Green Museum, London). The Rookwood Pottery founded in 1880 by Mrs. Nichols, the daughter of a wealthy Cincinnati family, because she was unable to find a suitable place elsewhere in which to conduct her experiments in china painting and under-glaze pottery decoration, soon became America's foremost art-pottery. Floral themes as used on this jar, continued to be the most characteristic during the 1890s.

111 *Vase decorated by A. R. Valentien* with dragons on an aventurine ground, Rookwood. 1898 (Bethnal Green Museum, London).

112 *Vase* decorated by Constance A. Baker with poppies on a black and brown ground, Rookwood. 1900 (Bethnal Green Museum, London).

113 *Bottle-shaped vase* decorated by K. Shirayamadani with a pattern of arrow flowers, Rookwood. 1900 (Victoria and Albert Museum, London). Mrs. Nichols had been personally inspired by the Japanese exhibit at the Centennial Exhibition at Philadelphia in 1876, and imported as one of the pottery's decorators the Japanese craftsman, Kataro Shirayamadani.